# Natalie
&

*Natalie*

By
Daniel Ragan

PublishAmerica
Baltimore

© 2012 by Daniel Ragan.
All rights reserved. No part of this book may be reproduced, stored in a retrieval system or transmitted in any form or by any means without the prior written permission of the publishers, except by a reviewer who may quote brief passages in a review to be printed in a newspaper, magazine or journal.

First printing

All characters in this book are fictitious, and any resemblance to real persons, living or dead, is coincidental.

PublishAmerica has allowed this work to remain exactly as the author intended, verbatim, without editorial input.

Softcover 9781462683192
PUBLISHED BY PUBLISHAMERICA, LLLP
www.publishamerica.com
Baltimore

Printed in the United States of America

# Table of Contents

Chapter 1..................................................7

Chapter 2................................................12

Chapter 3................................................23

Chapter 4................................................35

Chapter 5................................................50

Chapter 7................................................66

Chapter 8................................................78

Chapter 10............................................104

*This book is dedicated to Kate, Cecily, and Cherry.
May your friendship last forever.*

# Chapter 1

She really hadn't planned on things going as crazy as they had, but then life was kind of like that. If life threw you a curve you had to do your best to hit a homerun. In Natalie's case, she had let things get way out of control. But let's start at the beginning of the story, shall we? It began about a year ago, as Natalie Rashion; her best friend, Elizabeth Lancewood; and her cousin, Grace Rashion had all graduated from high school. So let us head back in time to that moment in Roscommon, Michigan, as Natalie, Elizabeth, and Grace all planned for their future.

It was a dreary rainy day, as Natalie lay sprawled out over her bed; Elizabeth slumped into a large bean bag chair in the corner, while Grace sat tinkering with Natalie's jewelry box, admiringly.

"So now that school is over, what's next?" asked Natalie, lifting her head from her bed.

Grace shrugged, uncaring. "Who knows? We'll all probably go off doing our own thing, get married, and have kids. You know, the usual." She answered.

"Oh, please. That sounds so horribly routine!" declared Elizabeth, chucking a pillow at Grace, playfully. "I want to do something great with my life. You know, like become the owner of my own photography company, or become a rich and famous person." said Elizabeth, looking off, as if in a daze.

"I want to get married to the most handsome man alive. Then we'll both get rich together." stated Grace, displaying a large artificial ruby ring on her finger.

"How about you Nat? What do you want to do with your life?" asked Elizabeth, ignoring Grace.

Natalie propped herself up on one elbow, "I want to travel the world. I want to meet adventure face to face!" she declared, enthusiastically. "I mean, wouldn't it be great to see amazing sights like the Eiffel Tower, or Big Ben and the Parliament Building? To be able to say 'I kissed the Blarney Stone of Blarney Castle.' Tour the Louver, walk the Palace of Versailles. Meet some incredibly handsome European gentlemen, poor *or* rich, and then spend the rest of our lives traveling! Wouldn't that be great?" she asked.

Elizabeth nodded her head in agreement.

"But that's so unrealistic!" whined Grace, bringing them all back to reality.

"Well, marrying the most handsome man alive is too." retorted Natalie, rolling her eyes, and laying back on her bed.

"But, seriously you guys, we could travel if we all wanted too! I mean we have all our graduating and open-house money, and if we pooled it all together plus our savings we could take a trip to Europe! How about it?" suggested Elizabeth.

Natalie and Grace both sat upright, suddenly very interested in what Elizabeth had said.

"You know, that might just be one adventure we could make happen!" said Natalie, a look of determination in her eyes.

The rest of the day was spent brainstorming on the idea. Grace, who was the romantic of the group suggested that they make it a summer vacation, and that they would see if their parents would allow them to first. Elizabeth, the brains of the bunch, suggested that they first see about funds, and *then* they would talk to their parents! Natalie, the dreamer of the bunch, agreed with both ideas. Thus the three girls began to plan out the rest of their summer.

Several weeks later, the girls were packed and ready to go, all of them at the airport with each one's parents saying goodbye. It had taken all of Natalie's canny persuasive ability to convince her parents to let her go, but in the end they had given her their consent.

"I want you to be very careful, Natalie!" instructed her dad, hugging her tightly.

"I will Dad, I promise." She said, squeezing him tightly in return.

"Have fun, Natalie. Be safe, and come home soon!" said her mom, a tear trickling down her cheek.

"Don't worry Mom; we'll be home in six weeks. I'll write to you guys when I get there." She said, hugging them both closely.

As Natalie walked toward the security check, her dad couldn't help but notice how fast she had become a beautiful young lady. It seemed like yesterday that she had been brought home from the hospital with that tiny little red bow in her light brown hair. Now here she was, nineteen years old, her hair long and dark brown, her brilliant hazel eyes shinning in the light, waving goodbye. His little girl had grown up.

Elizabeth, Grace, and Natalie had been friends since the 5$^{th}$ grade, and had practically grown up together. It had always been Elizabeth, though, that had been Natalie's *best* friend and confident. Not that she and Grace weren't friends, but because of the closeness as a cousin, they had always had their differences. Elizabeth, a year older than Natalie and Grace both, had bouncy brown hair with dark brown eyes, slightly shorter than Natalie, but taller than Grace. Grace, on the other hand, had light brown hair that hung down to her shoulders, and pale blue eyes.

As the girls boarded the plane, their emotions were flying high as their hearts pumped with excitement. Finally they were on their way! Adventure awaiting them, as their flight would land first in London, England, and after several weeks in London, they would then proceed to Paris, France. They had reserved a small flat to live in while they stayed in London. Each girl had chipped in an equal amount of money to share the rent. And after they got settled in, they would tour London's sights. Soon the plane was airborne, and the girls soon fell into a fitful sleep as the plane rocked gently over the Atlantic.

Shortly, Natalie drifted off into a strange dream. She was walking down the banks of the Thames River, as a young man came up to her and started chatting with her. She couldn't help but notice how cute he was as he spoke and smiled at her. Then he seemed to be making an annoying 'dinging' sound with his mouth, and suddenly his voice changed drastically to that of a woman's!

"Attention passengers, we are now making our descent to London National Airport. Please remain seated and belted at all times. Thank you for flying with Transcontinental Airlines." He said, staring Natalie in the face.

Instantly, her eyes flew open.

"Where am I?" she hissed, not recognizing her surroundings.

Elizabeth and Grace were both laughing at her as they explained that she had been asleep the entire flight over.

"Oh, I guess I was having a dream." Natalie replied, chuckling to herself.

What did her dream mean? Was it just her mind and wishful thinking? Or was it possibly a hint of things to come? She shook her head, as if to erase the dream as the plane began its descent.

# Chapter 2

About an hour later, the girls had finally made it through all the baggage checks and security passes, and were now looking to hail a taxi and make their way to their flat. As they walked out into the parking lot, they noticed a long black limousine parked along side the curb, a stiff English chauffer waiting at the passenger side. Seeing the car, the three girls stopped to admire it, and possibly get a glimpse of the owner.

"Wouldn't it be nice to be picked up in style like that?" sighed Grace, the other two girls nodding in agreement.

"I wonder how much it must have cost to rent that thing." asked Natalie, cynically.

"Maybe it's not a rental." suggested Elizabeth, beginning to walk away with her luggage.

Just then, the chauffer approached the three girls, all of them stopping and staring wide eyed.

"Miss Ragion?" he asked, bowing slightly.

"Uh, actually my name is Natalie Rashion." She pronounced slowly and articulately.

"Yes, Miss Natalie Ragion. I am John. I was sent to retrieve you to the hotel, although I was told it would only be you that I was to pick up." He introduced.

"Um, sir, I think there's some mistake. We're from America. We're not supposed to be picked up by any Limo!" insisted Elizabeth.

"Are you not Miss Natalie Ragion?" he asked, confused.

"I am Natalie Ray-she-on," she said pronouncing her name phonetically, "not 'Ragion'." She explained.

"Oh, that explains it!" he exclaimed, smiling, throwing back his head to laugh.

The girls all nodded, thinking he finally got it right.

"Since you've been schooled in America, I pronounced your last name with the original French pronunciation, whereas you with the American." He laughed.

Natalie let out an exasperated sigh. Grace instantly pulled Natalie aside for a moment, excusing herself from the chauffer.

"Are you out of your mind? This is perfect! Even if you're not this 'Ragion' chick, why not at least see what's going on? And if it turns out you're not who they expected, than we'll just say it was a simple mistake." She insisted.

By this time Elizabeth had come over too.

"And what if it's like illegal or something? We'd all end up in some English prison from here till doomsday!" Elizabeth rationalized.

"Oh, we will not! She'll...*we'll* be fine!" she declared.

"Let's at least see where he's taking us." replied Natalie, her curiosity now piqued.

With that, the girls turned around back to John.

"Um, where exactly were you supposed to take...me?" she asked.

"To the Grand London Hotel, where you are to be the guest of the Lord and Lady Granville. They have been anxiously awaiting your arrival, and are eager to see you." He explained.

"How do they know me?" she asked.

"They were very good friends with your parents before the accident." He said.

At that Grace piped up, "All right, we'll go at once! Would you mind helping us with our bags?" she asked.

As John went to work packing their bags into the back, Natalie and Elizabeth shot Grace a look that could kill.

"What in the world are you thinking? I've never heard of Lord and Lady Granville in my whole life! They'll know for sure I'm not this 'Ragion' girl!" whispered Natalie, climbing into the back of the limo.

"Not if we help you out." replied Grace. "Remember your dream that you said you wanted to do? Well, this could be it! Elizabeth and I will help you play the part of a rich royal, and find out all about this 'Natalie Ragion', and you can pretend to be her for a few weeks! I mean it's not like she's gonna show up. I doubt that she was even on the plane! It will be perfect." Grace cheered.

"I have to agree, it would be kind of fun to play that part, Nat." said Elizabeth.

Natalie nodded. "I suppose. But I just hope I don't get caught." She said.

"Its like I said, if we get caught we'll just say we didn't know." Grace replied.

And with that, John climbed in the front seat, and the three girls were off to the Grand London Hotel.

As the girls made their way through the busy London streets, John pointed out the many different sights of London; the Parliament Building, Big Ben, London Bridge, and the Royal Palace.

"So, Miss Ragion, this would only be your second trip into London, wouldn't it?" John asked, casually.

"Well, um...I don't quite remember. What time did *you* think I was here last?" stammered Natalie, glancing nervously between Elizabeth and Grace.

"Well, I think I was told that you lived near London about seventeen years ago, before your family moved, and you were sent to America for schooling." explained John.

"Oh! Right! Of course. I don't really remember that since it was so long ago, you know." Continued Natalie

"I guess you wouldn't, would you?" laughed John, "It's too bad about your parents. I was so sorry to hear about their car accident all those years ago. They were good people, Neville and Luciana. I was privileged to be their driver for a day. Nice people." said John, shaking his head.

"Yes, yes they were." Natalie nodded somberly, "It was really hard for me to be away for so long, but it *was* my parents wish that I be schooled in America." Natalie lied, feeling very skittish.

Elizabeth rolled her eyes, feeling a huge wave of guilt wash over her.

"Ah, here we are, ladies. The Grand London Hotel." announced John, pulling up to the massive building. "I'll go see about reservations, and we'll have one of the porters take up your bags. So, you ladies just wait here for a few moments." John insisted, parking the car near the entrance.

As he left, the girls rolled down their windows and peeked out at the gigantic hotel. The entrance had two large glass doors with gold plated door handles, while the hotel itself stretched a massive fifteen stories into the sky, each room with its own balcony and picture window.

"Holy Cow!" blurted out Natalie, her head sticking out of the Limo window, while Grace leaned her head out the opposite window, and Elizabeth stood through the skylight.

"Oh my word, look at the ladies dress! It's gorgeous!" said Grace, speaking much too loudly as an elderly rich couple walked past the limo.

"Honestly, Harold. You'd think those Americans would have better manners!" huffed the woman, tilting her nose up at the girls. "They look like a bunch of monkeys; the way they're sticking their heads out of that automobile!" she continued, loudly.

"Why you overstuffed, pig-headed, fat COW!" retorted Elizabeth, hearing the woman.

"I beg your pardon?" shrieked the woman, marching over to the limo. "Have you any idea who you're speaking to?" she demanded.

"Does it matter?" Natalie quipped.

"No matter who you are you can't go around making fun of people!" insisted Grace, joining in the fight.

"How *dare* you! I am the Lady Deuhurst! My husband is a Member of Parliament! You are merely American curs!" she said, curtly.

"Actually, Madame, you have the honor of addressing Miss Natalie Ragion of Devonshire." interjected John, returning at just the right time.

"What? The little English girl whose parents died and left her their entire fortune and estate?" piped up Lord Deuhurst.

"The very one. She's also one of the richest young royals in all of London." reminded John. Meanwhile, Natalie, Elizabeth, and Grace all sat staring at each other in shock. She was the richest girl in London?

"Do forgive me, young lady. But I can tend to be an old crank sometimes. I let my temper get the better of me. You girls will have to join us for tea tonight." Lady Deuhurst apologized.

"We'd love to, Madame." Natalie replied, speaking for the whole group.

"7:30 then? Will that do?" she asked.

"Perfect." replied all three girls at once.

With that, the Lord and Lady Deuhurst made their way into the hotel, as John escorted the three girls to their room.

"Here you are." He announced. John threw open the double doors to their room to reveal a very spacious room with three massive beds each with its own lace canopy; a kitchenette, and a patio that led to the balcony with three chairs under a white parasol. It looked so elegant, and it was all theirs! Natalie, Elizabeth, and Grace all marched into the room, trying to hide their amazement. It was John, who interrupted their thoughts,

"All right, I'll be back at 3:00 to take you to the Granville's mansion for luncheon. Do be ready; they hate to be kept waiting. See you then." He called, as he closed the door after him.

"Thanks, John." called Natalie, leaning out the door after him.

John waved as he entered the elevator. As soon as Natalie saw that he was gone, she ran back into the room and stopped at the door. She gave Elizabeth a very mischievous look before she sprinted for the bed and jumped onto it, bouncing up and down. Soon, the three of them were bouncing from bed to bed, giggling and shrieking, oblivious to all else. They were laughing so hard that they didn't hear the manager of the hotel knock at the door and come in to welcome Natalie to his hotel. As he entered, he merely stared in shock at the three girls bouncing all over the silken bed sheets. Elizabeth saw him first and desperately tried to get the other two girl's attention.

"I think the mouse is gone, girls!" she blurted out.

Natalie and Grace immediately stopped jumping, giving Elizabeth a quizzical look.

"What mouse?" laughed Natalie, plopping down on her bed.

But then she noticed the manager staring at them.

"Oh, hello there...sir. We thought we saw a...a...we thought we saw a..." she stammered, looking at Elizabeth and Grace for help.

"A mouse! Isn't that right, girls?" Elizabeth giggled nervously.

The manager suddenly became very nervous.

"A mouse? In *my* hotel? I'm terribly sorry ladies. I'll have your rooms changed at once! I was only coming in here to welcome Miss Ragion to the Grand London Hotel. And if any of you need anything, feel free to ask, compliments of the Hotel." He assured, trying to change topics from the mouse.

The three girls nodded, trying hard to suppress their laughter.

"Thank you. And also don't worry about the mouse. I'm sure it was just our over active imaginations. No need to change rooms. We like this one." Natalie smiled innocently.

The manager nodded and swiftly left the room, leaving the girls to bury their faces so as to stifle their hysterical laughter. It was Grace who settled them back down.

"Okay, seriously Nat. If you're gonna pull this off, you need to know everything about this girl, from her birth till now!" she urged. Natalie nodded, as Elizabeth plugged in her laptop and connected to the internet.

"Okay, Natalie Ragion. Born in Devonshire, England. Born to Neville and Luciana Ragion. Both parents now deceased in an automobile accident several years ago when she was fourteen years old. She was schooled at a private school in the

United States' mid-west region with a focus in art. Apparently the headmaster was a friend of the family's. She is the only surviving heir to her father's estate and two million pounds!" read Elizabeth in awe.

Natalie and Grace ran to either side of the computer and listened intently.

"Is there anything on her person? What she's like or how she acts?" asked Natalie. Elizabeth began scrolling down rapidly to a mini-biography of the heiress.

"Here it is! She's usually a quiet, reserved person; but very open with friends and family. Loves chocolate covered... prunes? Oh, that's gross." admitted Elizabeth, making a gagging face. "Also enjoys bicycling. Well, that's something to go off of." She suggested. Natalie sighed, wearily.

"How am I supposed to impersonate a girl that is quiet *and* eats chocolate covered prunes? I'll probably talk too much, puke up the prunes, and fall over on a bicycle! I haven't ridden a bike since like 7th grade!" Natalie confessed.

Grace quickly contradicted her, "Oh, come on! Just pretend you've given up your prunes, given up bicycling, and suddenly become more talkative." She recommended.

Elizabeth laughed, shaking her head. "You can't make her a completely different person, Grace! She's got to do it the right way. She can probably pull it off, but until John comes back, she has got to practice walking and acting like a spoiled rich heiress." instructed Elizabeth.

Grace quickly grabbed a couple of very large books from the room's library, placing them on Natalie's head.

"Okay, start walking!" she ordered.

Natalie gingerly took one little step, the books all cascading to the floor in a heap.

"Can I please start with a lighter book? I feel like I've got Webster's Dictionary stacked on top of a thesaurus! It's making me slouch!" she complained.

"Alright, fine. Practice sitting delicately."

Thus the girls continued practicing until it was time for Natalie to go. But half an hour before, they suddenly realized that she had no clothes that would do for the occasion!

"How could we have forgotten that?" demanded Grace, as Natalie began pacing in panic.

"Hold it girls. I have an idea! Let's call up Lady Deuhurst and have her send some up!" Elizabeth said, jumping at the phone.

Lady Deuhurst was very accommodating, and five minutes before departure time, Natalie was in her new dress. In her mind it was overly modern and fancy. It came just barely below the knee, the top climbing to her throat with no sleeves. The entire dress was a satin, scarlet color, topped off with a large, cherry-red, wide-brimmed hat that seemed to encompass her whole head and seemed to be just dripping with flowers

Suddenly, there was a knock at the door. Natalie jumped in alarm, clutching Elizabeth's hands frantically.

"Lizzie, I can't do this! What if I mess up?" she asked.

Elizabeth smiled, and hugged her friend tightly.

"You'll be fine. Too bad we can't go with you this time, but I assure you, you'll do fine." She said, as Grace opened the door.

As she did, in walked John with two very imposing men dressed in black suits and dark glasses.

"Hello again, Miss Ragion. This is Mr. James Butler, and Mr. Michael Masterly. His lordship, George Granville insisted that you have bodyguards assigned to you." explained John.

While Natalie stared at the two men in apprehension, Elizabeth and Grace stared at the men with admiration.

"Wow! They are *way* cute!" whispered Grace to Elizabeth. Elizabeth nodded her head in agreement.

"Pleased to meet you, ma'am." Mr. Butler greeted, extending his hand to Natalie. Natalie delicately shook his hand, remembering to play the part of the quiet, shy heiress.

"Thank you. These are my two best friends, Miss Elizabeth Lancewood and Grace…"

Natalie stopped, realizing that she couldn't admit to having Grace as a cousin!

"Grace Vanclick. Nice to meet you, sir." Grace interjected quickly using her mother's maiden name, and shaking his hand.

John hastily checked his watch, and glanced up at Natalie,

"If you are ready, Miss, we shall accompany you to the car." He said, bowing slightly.

Natalie nodded, and with a bodyguard on both sides and John in the front, Natalie began her charade, on her way to the Granville Mansion. But as she left the room, head held high, the wide brim of her massive hat got stuck between the door frames halting Natalie awkwardly. A high pitched giggle escaped from Lizzie, as she threw a hand over her mouth to cover it. After some maneuvering, and with help from John, Natalie managed to get through the door.

"Alright then?" he asked.

Natalie nodded, "Yes, quite. These hats can be such a nuisance." she added, glaring at Elizabeth and Grace who were stifling their laughter in the room. The two girls held thumbs up, wishing her the best.

But as Natalie walked down the hall, Elizabeth and Grace watched her slip both hands behind her back and cross her fingers. This was the real test.

# Chapter 3

Soon Natalie was traveling along in her private limo with her bodyguards on either side, sitting very still and quiet. The silence was just about killing Natalie. It wasn't like her to just sit and not say anything. She had to try and break the ice with these two Herculean men.

"So, um, why does Lord Granville think I need bodyguards?" she finally asked. James Butler responded first, "Well, since you've just recently inherited your parents' estate, he sees you as a possible target for others. You'd have no idea how many people get blackmailed for things like this." He explained.

Natalie nodded her head, pretending to be interested.

"So how long have you two been in the 'Protection' business?" she asked, prying. Michael Masterly's face remained stoic and impassive, while James Butler's broke out in a smile.

"I wouldn't call this the protection business, Ma'am. But I've been a personal bodyguard by employ of Lord and Lady Granville since I left Cambridge last fall." He explained.

Natalie's face lit up.

"Oh, so you're only about twenty-four or so?" she asked bluntly.

Butler grinned. "That is correct." He replied, suddenly catching a look from his partner.

"It is highly irregular for one to be so interested in one's servants, Ma'am." said Michael coldly.

Natalie blushed and realized her mistake.

"Oh, sorry. I just thought that since I was to be around you both for a while, that I'd get to know a little about you. I'm sorry if I've offended you, Mr. Masterly." She said quietly.

This at once had the effect she'd hoped for as Michael Masterly broke down into a half smile.

"Oh no, Miss. I guess I am a little bit of a stiff, as the yanks say." He chuckled. Natalie smiled, she seemed to have finally broken the ice between the two, and instantly felt much more at ease around them. For the remainder of the ride, each one grew to know the other more and more.

In about an hour, they pulled up to an exquisite mansion with large iron gates entwined with creeping vines and little rose buds crawling over them. Once through the gates, they rolled past the vibrant green lawn with an ornate fountain sparkling in the center. She saw several gardeners working diligently; pruning flowers, weeding gardens, and laying down mulch. Then she saw the house itself. It was a three story home with colossal marble pillars preceding the veranda.

As the limo pulled up to the front doors, several servants lined up outside the car awaiting her arrival. John smoothly parked the car, and opened Natalie's door. Natalie tried desperately not to stare at her surroundings as she walked up the marble steps into the house. Once inside, the head servant, or butler, requested her to wait till he had announced her arrival. Natalie nodded daintily, and seated herself on a plush Victorian style couch, Butler and Masterly standing on either side, hands crossed in front, looking like two statues.

Finally Natalie whispered, "I thought they knew I was coming."

Butler remained still, staring straight ahead and answered, "Perhaps you've forgotten since you were away in America, but it's customary when one enters someone's home to wait until one is announced. They do not merely enter without introduction." He whispered.

Natalie nodded, as if she had forgotten.

"Of course. I guess it's just that I've been away for so long that I've fallen out of habit with my English ways." She replied.

Butler curtly nodded as the butler re-entered the room.

"Lord and Lady Granville will see you now, Miss." He said in the stiffest English way possible.

Natalie rose and followed the man, both her bodyguards walking in step behind her. Soon Natalie came upon a room with a massive couch, and ornately decorated with all the little trinkets that make one rich. As she entered, she was greeted by two very warm smiles from an elderly couple sitting across the room from her.

"Darling Natalie. It's been *so* long." cried out the woman, rushing to give Natalie a large hug.

"Oh, Lady Granville, it's so good to see you again after all these years." Natalie said, blushing as she hugged the woman in return.

At that, Lady Gwendolyn Granville pulled back and smiled at Natalie. She was a rather tall woman of about fifty or so. She had big white hair that was neatly done up and had thick make-up on, so as to best hide her age. She was plump, but she was also certainly a friendly looking woman, Natalie thought. She made one want to become instant friends with her. And her husband was of equal dignity. Although he was not quite as plump as his wife, he was equally as tall, with gently combed grey hair with dashes of black mixed in. He had on a royal blue suit with an ornate walking stick, and looked every bit the part of a lord.

"Oh, George, doesn't she look beautiful! Our dear friend's little baby all grown up and gorgeous!" cooed Lady Granville.

Lord Granville nodded his agreement as he too gave Natalie an affectionate hug.

"She certainly does, Gwendolyn. She certainly does. It's very good to see you Natalie. I trust you had a good flight over?" he asked, giving her a seat next to his wife and him.

"I did, your lordship. It was very pleasant." Natalie replied, shyly.

At this, Lady Granville laughed a big hearty laugh.

"Oh darling, you needn't call us lordship! You are permitted to refer to us as Uncle George and Aunt Gwendolyn. Like you used to!" she giggled, pressing her hand to Natalie's.

"Of course. I'm sorry. It's just that I've been away for so long that I seem to have forgotten so much, you know." She laughed lightly in return.

"I see you've picked up on the American accent." laughed Lady Granville, "I'm sure it'll fade in time."

A slight silence fell on the group, and Lord Granville's face suddenly lit up,

"Ah, you must be starved. While we wait for luncheon to be prepared, how would you like a chocolate covered prune?" he asked.

Natalie's heart sank. She had hoped they wouldn't ask her, but now she was doomed to try one. He genially held out a silver tray covered with the delicacy. Natalie hesitated for a few brief seconds. The chocolate covered prunes were enormous! They looked almost like squishy chestnuts, but she was sure they tasted far worse.

"Oh, come now! Don't tell me that our little girl has out grown her favorite snack?" asked Lady Gwendolyn.

Natalie smiled half-heartedly.

"No, no, no. It's just that…well; I don't want to ruin my appetite. I suppose I *will* take just one. These things can go straight to your middle." Natalie said, reaching out and plucking up one of the horrid little candies.

She quickly popped one into her mouth and tried to swallow it. But Natalie had not counted on the prune being as big as it was, and immediately began to gag.

"Oh good heavens! That was quite a bite!" exclaimed Lady Granville, lightly thumping Natalie's back.

Natalie frantically managed to swallow it in the end.

"Oh, that was delicious." Natalie wheezed, desperately trying to catch her breath.

"Oh, well in that case have another. We ordered boxes of them just for you!" Lady Granville offered, extending the tray to her.

Natalie almost gagged again, but just then a servant entered and announced lunch. Natalie instantly stood to her feet, followed by Lord Granville and James Butler and Michael Masterly.

"Good. I'm famished." She said smiling happily.

She had forgotten that in formal circles the men stood whenever a lady stood or entered a room. She knew she'd have to remember that, so as not to have all the men around her springing to their feet every time she stood up.

Natalie managed lunch with very little difficulty. Besides the fact that she almost spewed her vichyssoise (soup served cold) out of her mouth! They had chatted happily just like old friends. They had talked about her schooling and her two friends that she had brought along with her. Then came the most important topic of all; the estate!

"Now my dear, I'm sure that you are fully aware that someday you would inherit your parent's estate. Well, according to your father's wishes, I was given power of attorney over the affairs of his estate. Now, as you have returned to England, I have needed to discuss business with you." began Lord Granville. Natalie listened intently.

"You are to inherit everything; the house, the servants, the property, and the money. Yes, all two million pounds of it." Smiled Lord Granville as Natalie gasped a little. "He left important instructions that you receive it all at your eighteenth birthday. And since you have already passed into your nineteenth, than all that is to be done is for me to retrieve the deed of ownership from the vault at my bank, and for you to sign it. This of course may take several days while I proceed with all the formalities and such, so we will go ahead and allow you to remain at the Grand London Hotel. And after we have you sign the deed, you may immediately move into the estate." explained Lord Granville.

Natalie sat stunned, but tried to hide it.

"Thank you so much for handling all this, Uncle George. I'd have been lost if you hadn't." Natalie said, pressing her hand into her 'Uncle's.'

"All that we ask in return is that you throw a ball the first week you're home!" insisted Lady Granville. "We simply must show you off to all our old friends! Oh, and Ian will be home then too! You remember Ian, don't you dear?" asked Lady Granville.

Natalie sat confused, "Um, Ian? That would be…" she let her sentence trail off.

"Ian. You know our son? You two used to play together as children." She reminded.

Natalie nodded her head.

"Oh, I remember him. I had forgotten all about him. It's been years since I've seen him." She explained.

"Well, he's grown into quite a young man, my dear." said Lady Granville, smiling with a hint of mischief in her smile.

"He's been away at the academy for almost a year now. He'll be so pleased to see you again." said Lord Granville.

Natalie suddenly had yet another thing to be nervous about. Lady Granville was trying to set her up with her son! A son that was supposed to have been an old playmate, but a person that Natalie had never laid eyes on! Finally the lunch was done, and Natalie insisted that she really must get back to her hotel.

"I really do appreciate your hospitality, but I must be going. I promised Lord and Lady Deuhurst that I'd join them for tea after dinner tonight." Natalie excused.

"Oh, you've met the Deuhursts? Lovely people. Simply wonderful! Although a bit nosey. We used to be on terrible terms with them, but now we're quite civil. You'll have to invite them to the ball too!" prattled Lady Granville giddily. Natalie promised that she would, and excused herself after giving both people a hug and made her way to her limo.

Soon Natalie was back at the hotel with an ice pack on her head.

"I'm telling you both, I cannot do this anymore! I'm getting a terrible headache from trying to remember all these names and dates, and all this protocol!" Natalie said, wearily.

But Elizabeth and Grace wouldn't listen to her.

"Natalie, you've got to quit telling yourself this. You already pulled off the hardest part. Now who knows, maybe you were intended to become the owner of a rich estate." said Grace, fixing her hair.

"Oh no! Don't you dare even think of that! What if the real Natalie comes back just as I'm signing the deed? Then what?" Grace was about to reply, when Natalie continued, "I'll tell you what'll happen. I'll get carted off to the Tower of London and sit there and rot to death wondering why I ever listened to you two maniacs in the first place!" she yelled.

During all this, Elizabeth and Grace had been busy getting themselves ready for something.

"Where are you two going?" Natalie asked as her temper cooled.

Elizabeth quickly walked to one side of Natalie while Grace walked to the other.

"Up we go!" they both cried, as they hoisted her out of her chair.

"But…" Natalie tried to interject.

"We're going shopping! Now let's get you ready!" Elizabeth replied authoritatively.

Natalie sighed, and went into the other room to change. She knew trying to reason with her friends was hopeless.

Soon Natalie, Elizabeth, and Grace were busily going from store to store, getting the most expensive looking clothes, and charging it all to Natalie Ragion, whose reputation and money preceded her. After about an hour's worth of trying on multiple outfits, the girls decided to get a bite to eat. They soon found their way to a ritzy little café near the London Bridge, and each one got their first taste of English cuisine.

"So, you think you'll be able to pull off this ball thing?" asked Elizabeth, munching on a croissant roll.

Natalie sighed and sipped her tea.

"I hope so. But most of all, I hope this Ian guy doesn't have like some recent picture of this chick in his wallet or something. He'll be the first to know if it's not me." Natalie said.

Grace didn't even bother to pay any attention to the conversation as she played with the string of pearls she had bought that day. She was eagerly eyeing the male scenery.

"Why aren't there any cute guys checking me out?" she pouted.

Natalie was half tempted to expound on that fact, but Elizabeth flashed her a warning look, trying hard not to laugh as well.

"Well, we have to go back at the hotel soon. We'd better get going, huh?" said Elizabeth, placing a generous tip for their waiter.

But Natalie wasn't quite ready to return home yet. She and the girls decided to take a quiet stroll across the London Bridge and take in the scenery.

They soon left the café, and began the walk across the bridge. The night air was crisp and cool, and the stars were just starting to peek out one by one. The Parliament Building was all aglow along with Big Ben, and Natalie was drinking in the London atmosphere.

"I absolutely love it here." She murmured, staring out across the Thames River. But Elizabeth and Grace were freezing and started on again, walking on ahead. Natalie watched as they left, and actually appreciated being left alone to her thoughts for a while. And as she stood staring out into the city, the sound of water rushing below her, she did not hear the man come up behind her and clasp his hand over her mouth. Natalie felt panic rushing up into her throat.

"Hold still, love. All I want is yer purse!" he growled into her ear.

Natalie desperately thought of something to do, and swiftly brought her spiked heel down on the man's toe, taking a step away from the man. In anguish, the man cried out and brought his hand up to strike her, when all of a sudden another man grabbed his wrist.

"That's not very nice." He chided before bringing his fist up into the man's nose. The man crumpled under the blow, and was soon sprawled out on the pavement. "You alright, Miss?" asked the young man.

As he walked over to Natalie who sat shivering and trembling in the corner, she finally got a glimpse of the man's face. He was a handsome young man about her age. He had thick brown hair that was neatly combed and long sideburns. His deep blue eyes caught Natalie's, and she stared into them in wonder.

"I'll be alright...I think." She finally stammered.

"Ah, you're a yank?" he stated, but then quickly corrected himself, "Sorry. I meant you're an American." He said, smiling sheepishly.

Natalie loved the look of that smile and soon found herself smiling back.

"Yes, I am. Well, sort of. I suppose I'm not." She said, stumbling over her words. The man laughed.

"Well which is it? You either are or you aren't. Me, I'm a Brit." He said proudly.

"Well, I'm English, but I've lived in America for most of my life." She explained, assuming the part of the heiress.

Then for the first time, the young man seemed to recognize her.

"Wait, what's your name?" he asked, handing back her purse.

Natalie smiled impishly. "You first." She insisted.

At that the man laughed again.

"Ooh, a mystery woman, huh?" he joked. "Well, that's fine. I suppose you're entitled to your secret. So maybe I'll just keep my name a secret too." He grinned.

"Well, I really do thank you for saving me. I usually have a man with me, but I left him back at the car." She explained.

At this, the young man's countenance seemed to drop ever so slightly. Of course a lovely young woman like this *would* already have a man.

"Oh, then I must be keeping you. Forgive me. It was a pleasure to be of assistance. But I too must bid you farewell." He said, bowing low, and picking up his diamond studded walking stick in his leather gloves.

"Goodbye." Natalie said, as she watched the handsome stranger walk away into the darkness of the opposite side of the bridge.

She sighed a regretful sigh. Maybe she should have told him her name. That way she could've found out his name. Just then Elizabeth and Grace came running up with Michael Masterly and James Butler.

"Where have you been? We turned around expecting you to be right there with us, but you were gone!" cried out Grace. Then, spotting the unconscious mugger on the ground behind Natalie, Grace gasped loudly. "Natalie, what did you do?"

"Oh, well I was getting mugged." retorted Natalie.

Elizabeth gasped.

"It wasn't wise of you three to go shopping alone." insisted Butler.

"If you please, we really should get back to the automobile, Miss." ordered Masterly.

Natalie nodded, and while they drove, she relayed the story of her rescue to her two friends.

"Oh Natalie! That must have been terrible. I'm so sorry." Elizabeth apologized, sympathetically.

"Sorry nothing! It must have been wonderfully romantic!" said Grace, clasping her hands together melodramatically.

"Oh brother." mumbled Elizabeth.

But Natalie merely smiled. It had been romantic *and* horrible at the same time. But the worst thing was that Natalie now had no idea how to find her mysterious stranger again.

# Chapter 4

As the girls all tumbled into their rooms, they hastily dumped all their newfound boxes and bags of clothes all over the floor.

"I'm beat!" exclaimed Grace, dropping her pile directly in front of Elizabeth and Natalie. "I never knew shopping could be so exhausting." She complained.

Natalie and Elizabeth smirked.

"Provided you actually *do* some shopping. All you did was complain about how your feet were killing you all day. Try acting as someone you're not, shopping for hours, then getting mugged. It's a real ball!" retorted Natalie.

Grace ignored Natalie's remarks and quickly got ready for bed.

"Look Natalie, I know this is hard, but you *are* kind of stuck in this role now. Unless we can find the real Natalie Ragion, you'll end up in bigger trouble than you are now." Elizabeth insisted.

Natalie nodded in response.

"I know. I know. Tomorrow morning I'm going to look her up and see what I can find out about her. If I don't find her quickly, I'll be stuck playing this girl forever." Natalie complained.

But just then, Grace piped up,

"Oh, sorry Natalie. You can't do that tomorrow morning. You're supposed to play croquet with the Deuhursts at 9:00." She corrected.

"Excuse *me*?" asked Natalie fuming.

Grace smiled as if nothing were wrong.

"Yes. Madame Deuhurst called and left a message requesting you to come by tomorrow morning at nine. I took the liberty of calling her and confirming the date. Hope you don't mind." She added sweetly.

Natalie huffed in frustration.

"Grace, I am getting myself deeper and deeper into this charade, and all you can think about is playing the part to the fullest! You can't do this to me!" she insisted.

"Oh stop being so melodramatic, Nat. Just let me handle this by myself. It'll be fine. Let Lizzie look for this girl while you play the part. Besides, John called too and said that the press wants a statement after your game with the Deuhursts." She chattered. Natalie's eyes grew large as she approached her cousin threateningly. Grace gulped, throwing up her hands in defense. "Don't kill me! I'm your cousin, remember? You love me?" she squealed.

Natalie let out a long, exasperated sigh and slumped onto the bed.

"I give up." She muttered.

\*\*\*\*\*\*\*\*\*\*\*\*

The next morning dawned bright and beautiful for the three girls. And while Elizabeth rang for breakfast, Grace helped Natalie pick out a suitable outfit for croquette.

"Here. This would look ravishing! Don't you think?" chirped Grace, placing a huge spring hat with rose buds hanging all over it.

"Grace, I'm playing croquet. I'd rather not look like a sail boat with a radar dish attached to my head." Natalie pointed out.

"Quite right. But you must wear these. They're so dainty." She said handing her a pair of shoes.

Natalie looked at Grace in unbelief.

"These are high-heels!" she cried.

"Well, I'm glad you noticed. Of course they're heels!" she retorted.

"Grace, have you ever played croquet?" asked Natalie. Grace nodded. "And do you know where or *how* people play croquet?" Natalie asked again.

Grace shook her head dismissively.

"Croquet, golf, cricket; it's all the same. Whack a ball and see how far it goes, right?" Grace replied, rummaging through a box of gloves.

"Grace, croquet is played in the grass. In the GRASS! If I wear those shoes, I'll sink into the ground!" Natalie said, smoldering.

Grace then saw her point.

"Fine. Use these hideous plain flat shoes." grumbled Grace. "But you have to wear a hat." She scolded.

Just then breakfast was served, and all three girls sat down and ate hungrily. After the girls had finished breakfast, the phone rang, shattering the silence.

"Hello?" answered Elizabeth.

"Hello my dear. Is Natalie about? This is Lady Deuhurst calling." came the sophisticated voice at the other end.

Elizabeth handed the phone to Natalie, and went straight to her computer. She knew that Natalie didn't want to be stuck in this role any longer than she had to be, so it was up to her to find this 'Natalie Ragion' and bring her back to her rightful place.

"Hello Lady Deuhurst. Yes, I'm just about ready for croquet. Thank you. I'll meet you there. Alright. Goodbye." Natalie said hanging up the phone.

Then, she quickly prepared herself, rang up her two body guards, and was escorted to the garage where John waited with the car.

Meanwhile, back up in the hotel room, Elizabeth and Grace (mostly Elizabeth) dug up more information on Natalie Ragion.

"Where are you, Natalie?" mumbled Elizabeth aloud. Hastily she typed in what she already knew about her and hit search on the web.

All the while, Grace tried on the various outfits she had purchased the previous evening, not even worried about Elizabeth's problems.

"I still don't see why we have to find this girl." Complained Grace, trooping into the room flaunting a shocking pink boa.

Elizabeth rolled her eyes, both at the boa and her attitude.

"Why can't Natalie just be satisfied with her lot in life? It can't be *that* bad to be stuck as a rich heiress. I mean, if it gets old, she can just smile and insist that she didn't mean to. It'll be easy." She replied.

Elizabeth finally had had enough.

"Look Grace, the three of us have been friends for a long time. I think you of all people should sympathize with your cousin. Would you want to live out your life deceiving everyone?" She snapped.

Grace immediately looked over at her friend who had spoken with such force to her. Grace blushed slightly, while trying to appease her friend.

"Uh...well, I'm sorry. I guess I didn't think of it that way, Lizzie. I just was having so much fun with this that I didn't think to look at it from Natalie's point of view. Sorry." She said quietly and humbly.

Elizabeth nodded her head,

"That's alright. But let's just concentrate on finding this girl, and getting us out of London!" declared Elizabeth, scanning her laptop thoroughly.

Grace agreed, and the two of them went to work.

Elsewhere, John had just arrived at the beautiful country park where Natalie was to play a mid-morning game of croquet with the Deuhursts. But the entire ride over, she felt terribly guilty. How long could she keep up this charade? Eventually she'd have to go home. But how could she tell all these people, who were so sure that she was Natalie Ragion, that she wasn't? It would not only hurt them, but anger them! She hoped that Elizabeth could actually locate the real Natalie before she got too far into this role.

"Ah, how lovely you look, my dear." greeted Lord Harold Deuhurst, genially. Natalie smiled, as he escorted her to the croquette grounds where awaited Lady Madeline Deuhurst.

"I'm so happy you could make it, dear. I'll bet you haven't played croquet in years." She said handing Natalie a large wooden mallet.

"That's for sure." Natalie replied sweetly, fingering the mallet. *"In fact I've never played at all!"* she thought to herself.

"Well, I'm sure you're familiar with the rules, so no sense wasting more time. You go first, Natalie dear." insisted Lady Deuhurst.

Natalie smiled nervously as she walked up to the ball sitting dauntingly in the grass. Just then, Grace's words echoed in her mind…

*"Croquet, Golf, Cricket; it's all the same. Whack a ball and see how far it goes, right?"*

Natalie took a deep breath, brought her mallet up high, and swung with all her might. She couldn't have connected any better, as the mallet sent the heavy ball soaring through the air and straight into a couple's picnic basket nearby. With a loud thud, the ball landed smack in the middle of their food.

"I say, that was a ruddy nasty trick!" shouted the young man angrily. "What do you think this is? Golf?" he snapped.

Natalie turned to the Deuhursts, smiling sheepishly.

"Oh dear." whispered Lady Deuhurst. "Perhaps we **should** go over the rules again." She said, turning to her husband.

But Natalie had had enough.

"No, please don't waste your time. There's something I need to tell both of you." Natalie pleaded, turning earnestly to the Deuhursts.

The Deuhursts looked nervously at one another.

"Well, go ahead my dear. We're listening." insisted Lady Deuhurst.

Natalie took a deep breath before beginning.

"Well, first of all, I'm not Natalie Ragion." She stated, trying to break eye contact with the couple.

Lady Deuhurst gasped in surprise.

"How can this be? You're the right age, the right height, even the same face!" she blurted out.

But immediately, Lord Deuhurst stopped her. Natalie blushed deeply.

"Look, I tried to tell John that it was a mistake, but he insisted that I was confused, arguing over pronunciation of my last name. So, reluctantly, my cousin and friend convinced me to play the part for a while. I'd no idea it would get this difficult. I'm very sorry." She apologized earnestly.

Lord and Lady Deuhurst eyed each other carefully before answering her.

"Well, no harm done. If it was merely a misunderstanding, we'll forgive you." answered Lord Deuhurst smiling broadly.

Natalie sighed gratefully.

"You won't tell anyone will you?" she asked perplexed.

Lady Deuhurst smiled ever so sweetly.

"Oh, heavens no! What do you take us for? Gossips? No, it'll be our secret, my dear. But out of curiosity, what happened to the real Natalie?" she asked.

"Well, to be honest, I don't know. We figured she'd show up by now, but we haven't heard a thing. Right now my friend Elizabeth is trying to track her down via the internet." explained Natalie.

Lord Deuhurst nodded knowingly.

"Do you think I should tell everyone? I feel terrible living a lie." Natalie admitted. But Lady Deuhurst hurriedly stopped her.

"Oh, don't do that!" she practically shouted. "That would only cause problems. You understand, don't you?" she giggled.

Natalie looked confused, not sure what to do.

"I tell you what, Natalie, it is Natalie isn't it?" asked Lord Deuhurst. Natalie nodded. "We'll do the looking, while you continue with your charade. If we can't find her within two months, we'll let you go home. But if we do find her before than, we'll discreetly trade places with you. Agreed?" proposed Lord Deuhurst.

Natalie thought to herself, thinking over the consequences of her actions.

"Agreed. And thank you both so much." She said shaking their hands thankfully.

"Oh no, thank you." inserted Lady Deuhurst. "What say we put this game on hold for now? That way you can tell your friends the plan." She suggested.

Natalie agreed, and made her way back to the unsuspecting John, Michael and James.

Meanwhile, still back at the croquette course, Lord and Lady Deuhurst watched her as she drove off. As she did, Lord Deuhurst smiled to his wife.

"Isn't this an interesting turn of events, my dear?" he asked.

Lady Deuhurst smiled back cattily.

"To say the least, darling. The little heiress is *still* missing. This puts us in an interesting position, don't you think?" she asked still smiling.

Lord Deuhurst laughed.

"Why whatever do you mean my dear? You couldn't be referring to the incident with the 'dearly departed Ragions' now could you?" he said sarcastically.

But suddenly Lady Deuhurst became deathly serious.

"Seriously though Harold, this is our chance! We can still carry out our plan! If it hadn't been for those idiot Granville's with all their influence and money, we'd have had the estate by now!" complained Lady Deuhurst.

"Yes, it was unfortunate that he was given power of attorney. But that's about to change. If we find the real Natalie and expose the other as a fake, that should be sufficient evidence for the courts to take the power of attorney away from George

Granville, and pass it to the next in line. Me." laughed Lord Deuhurst wickedly.

"With you as attorney, we can manipulate thousands of pounds from the little brat!" schemed Lady Deuhurst.

"Well, we'd better be going. There is much to be done if we're to find the missing heiress." stated Lord Deuhurst coldly.

With that, he and Lady Deuhurst climbed into their Rolls Royce and sped off for their villa.

Soon Natalie was back in her hotel room and relaying the 'good news' to Elizabeth and Grace.

"...so that's it. Until the Deuhursts find Natalie Ragion, I'm her." Natalie finished.

Elizabeth nodded happily.

"At least now there's an end to this charade. Maybe we can still manage to see the rest of Europe. Maybe you'll even find the man of your dreams." teased Elizabeth, poking Natalie in the ribs.

The two of them laughed, except Grace.

"I still can't *believe* you told them!" she insisted. "You had it all, Natalie!"

Elizabeth shot Grace a disapproving look,

"I thought we settled that, Grace?" she snapped.

Instantly, Grace shut up.

"Fine, but can we still have the ball?" she whined.

Natalie looked at Elizabeth.

"I suppose. It might be fun at that. Besides, the Granville's will be expecting it. Yes, we will still have the ball Grace. In fact you can help me plan for it; both of you." Natalie planned.

Suddenly, Grace's eyes were full of life and excitement.

"Let's make it a masquerade ball!" she suggested.

The other two girls looked intrigued at the suggestion.

"Alright. A masquerade ball it is." Natalie stated simply.

The rest of the day was spent planning out details for the ball. But at about 6:00 that evening, John knocked lightly at Natalie's door.

"Oh, hi, John. Want to come in?" Natalie asked, answering the door.

But John shook his head no,

"Actually, I came to tell you that your press conference is in half an hour. I thought maybe you had forgotten." He reminded.

Natalie immediately turned very pale.

"Oh darn." She said simply. "Uh, look John, could you send Michael and James up to my room please? I need to talk to them. And don't worry about the press, I'll be ready." She promised, closing the door abruptly in his face.

Instantly Natalie turned to face the other girls, a scream building in her throat.

"Just keep calm. We'll figure out something, trust me." Elizabeth said to Natalie. "Grace, go find her something to wear for the conference. Something exquisite, but suitable." Elizabeth added.

Grace nodded and darted off for the closet and began pulling off various gowns and hats and gloves and skirts from off the hangers. Meanwhile Natalie tried to rack her brains for a plan.

"Maybe the guys can help us out." Suggested Grace to Elizabeth.

"What? You mean those two bodyguards? What can they do to help?" demanded Elizabeth.

"Who cares? I just like having two cute guys guarding me!" she said, poking her head around the corner of the closet.

Elizabeth huffed and ignored her.

"No, really Elizabeth. They might give me some pointers." Natalie insisted waving her hand around frantically.

Just then a loud knock was heard behind Natalie, making her jump.

"Here they are." said Natalie.

Instantly, Elizabeth squealed and darted from the room in order to change and fix her hair, pulling Grace along with her.

"Oh brother!" moaned Natalie, opening the door. "Hi guys. Come in." she greeted, ushering the two large men inside. "Look, I need your help. I'm supposed to do this press conference, but I've no idea what to say or how to say it." She sighed exasperated.

James Butler sat back thinking while Michael Masterly answered first.

"How about we feed you the words? If you wore one of our ear pieces, we could communicate to you unawares." He suggested.

Natalie's face lit up.

"That's a great idea! You could get Elizabeth and Grace to help out too!" she replied.

Just then Elizabeth and Grace walked in, blushing deeply at the sight of the two men, and the two men turned red right back.

"Sounds like a plan to me." said James, staring at Elizabeth.

Elizabeth tried to hide her smile by biting her lip, but couldn't and instead managed to just hurt her lip.

"Ow." she whispered, hoping desperately that he hadn't noticed.

So for the next half hour, James and Michael, with the girls help, fitted one of the ear phones into Natalie's ear and hid the wire in a braid of Natalie's hair. Then with the remaining time, Natalie rushed to get ready. The dress Grace had picked out was perfect. It was a magnificent blue suit-coat top with a fresh rose in her lapel. Then she wore an ebony black skirt with equally dark spiked heels. Her hair was put up with two braids holding it in place, with a stylish blue and black purse slung over her shoulder. She was ready.

Once everything was done, Natalie was escorted by John to the lobby while Masterly and Butler along with Elizabeth and Grace made their way to the outside of the lobby, standing in the doorway. As Natalie came into the room, she was shocked. Flash bulbs popped in her face blinding her, people chattered incessantly, and Natalie felt overwhelmed.

Into her mic, she whispered, "I don't think I can do this."

But as she looked over at the bodyguards, they gave her a reassuring thumbs up. Natalie sighed and took the platform.

"Hello everybody." She said loudly, the microphone ringing with feedback.

The room fell silent.

"I am Natalie Ragion, and I'd like to thank everyone for coming to welcome me home." She began.

Instantly she was flooded with questions.

"Uh...one at a time, please. You sir." said Natalie, pointing to one of the journalists.

"Miss Ragion, does it feel strange calling England your home after being in America for so long?" asked the man.

Without waiting for a prompt from her bodyguards, Natalie launched into her own spiel.

"Regardless of the fact that I lived in America for so long, I'll always consider England my true home. After all, it is the land of the free, and the home of the brave." She stated grandly.

An awkward silence filled the room. Elizabeth bit her lip again nervously.

"I think she's been away a little *too* long." whispered James to Elizabeth.

"Next question." Natalie urged hesitantly.

"Miss Ragion, now that you've inherited your parent's estate, what will you do with all that money?" asked a young female journalist.

Natalie smiled and this time waited for a prompt.

"Say that you'll try to use it for as much good as possible." prompted Michael.

"I should like to try and use it for as much good as possible." Natalie replied.

Her answer was well received as journalists scribbled frantically on their pads.

"Miss Ragion, do you have plans of getting married now that you're home to stay?" asked another.

But before Natalie could get a response from her bodyguards, someone bumped the two men standing in the doorway, knocking their microphones from their ears!

"Dreadfully sorry about that!" apologized the woman that had done it.

Without thinking, Natalie answered,

"Dreadfully sorry..." but then realized her mistake. "I'm not...no answer, or comment. Whatever it is people say when they don't want to answer." She stuttered.

The journalists chuckled and moved to the next question.

"Miss Ragion, there is a rumor that you'd like to hold a ball as a homecoming party, is that true?" asked another man.

By this time, the bodyguards had fixed their problem and had their ear phones back in place, but unfortunately they had missed the question!

"What did they ask?" whispered James to Grace.

Grace too had missed it, but thought she had heard something else.

"Something about an 'arty'. Whatever that is." Grace shrugged.

But James nodded his head.

"I'll bet their talking about art." He replied, and fed Natalie her next line.

"I'm not terribly fond of art, but I do enjoy some paintings and etchings. I'm quite an avid lover of Van Gogh and De Vinci though." She replied.

The journalists looked bewildered.

"Does that answer your question, sir?" Natalie asked sweetly.

The man merely stared and replied, "Uh...not really."

"Anyways, next?" Natalie urged. But as she was bombarded with more questions, interference in the ear-piece kept buzzing in and out.

"What was your favorite part of living in the US?" one reporter asked. Natalie waited for a cue from her men, but instead got the last bit of someone's fast-food order buzzing into her ear-piece.

"I'd like the fish and chips combo." she stated. The room chuckled as Natalie blushed. "Sorry. Don't know where *that* came from." she laughed nervously. "Sometimes random things just pop into my head." she rambled on. Then she caught her bodyguards' eyes along with Grace and Elizabeth. "But I really wish they wouldn't." she emphasized. The crowd glanced around at each other, clearly confused, but they pressed on.

Finally, the conference was coming to an end.

"Thank you all for your time, and be sure to attend the ball I plan on having. Thank you all." She said, waving gracefully.

In her mind it had all gone smoothly, but in fact it was a disaster! Stepping off the platform, Natalie breathed a sigh of relief.

"Well, overall that went well. Don't you think?" Natalie asked innocently.

Elizabeth merely grabbed Natalie's arm with Grace on the other side.

"You're going to need a lot more work. Let's go." she instructed, sounding very motherly.

Dazed and confused, Natalie followed behind, leaving a very confused mass of journalists and reporters.

# Chapter 5

Meanwhile, the Deuhursts were alive with excitement. They finally had the chance they had been waiting for after so many years.

"The ignorant fool! She's played right into our hands unwittingly. Even *we* didn't realize she wasn't the real Natalie. Now, using whatever means necessary, we must find the real Natalie and replace her with this American." chattered Lady Deuhurst, wafting around the room happily.

"My dear, please curb your excitement. First we have to actually *find* her. It could be harder than you think." replied Lord Deuhurst calmly puffing on a cigarette held in an elegant cigarette holder. "I've already sent out private investigators to locate the young girl. She apparently was last sighted leaving Las Angeles in a large party of young people. Our first thought was that she going on a college outing, but we're still not sure. My man will get back with me before the week is over. Until then, we must keep up pretences with this girl. I need you to be her closest confident, know her dreams, her goals. Set her up for the biggest fall of all time. Then, when the time is right, and when we have the girl, we will reveal her for the fraud she really is!" schemed Lord Deuhurst.

Lady Deuhurst cackled in glee. "Oh Harold, my darling, you are incredibly wicked!" she giggled. "This is going to be marvelous. All that 'cash', to put it in the American vernacular." she smiled. Lord Deuhurst grinned in return, wrapping his arms around his wife and wrapping her in his embrace.

Elsewhere, Lady Granville stood impatiently waiting on the balcony sipping her tea periodically. After a while the sound of a door opening caught her attention.

"Ian, is that you, dear?" asked Lady Granville.

"Hello Mother." said Ian strolling into the room.

He casually tossed his black leather gloves and walking stick to the nearby butler who caught them deftly, and hugged and kissed his mother.

"Darling, where have you been? I really wish you wouldn't make it a habit to go off gallivanting into the night on wild excursions. We have our family honor to uphold." she reprimanded sweetly, kissing his cheek.

Ian sighed and sunk into one of the plush leather chairs.

"Don't worry, Mother, I made it a point to rob only rich people we *don't* know, so if I get caught, they won't know who I am." he said sarcastically.

Lady Granville looked horrified.

"Ian, that's not funny! Tell me you didn't do something foolish again. Please, darling, we can't afford another scandal. That last one was quite enough. Hitchhiking all over Europe dressed as a beggar. Honestly, I don't know what possessed you to do it." she huffed, seating herself gently in her armchair.

Ian laughed as he recalled his last great escapade.

"No, Mother, I did nothing of the sort. In fact, you would have been proud of me last night. I did something good." he said proudly, leaning his head back in his chair. Lady Granville looked concerned.

"Why is it then when you say something like that, I feel as if I'm in for a shock?" she asked nervously.

But Ian shook his head.

"No, really Mother, I'm not fooling around. Last night after the play, I went for a walk along the London Bridge. It was there that I came across a young woman getting mugged." he began.

"Oh, Ian, you didn't! You didn't take on a mugger, did you?" she asked aghast.

"Yes, I did. I beat the man trying to steal the girl's purse, and returned the purse to its owner. Who, if I do say so myself, was quite a beautiful young girl, at that." he added, smiling to himself.

Lady Granville rolled her eyes and rose from her chair.

"Oh, no you don't. Not this time, Ian. I've had to bail you out of one to many messy relationships with greedy young women, and I **will *not*** do it again. You will marry a respectable young lady, and you will honorably carry on the Granville legacy!" she scolded, setting her cup of tea down.

Ian turned angrily at his mother.

"You know, that's all I've ever heard from you and Father since I was old enough to notice girls. What if I don't want to 'carry on the Granville legacy'?" he retorted. "What if I actually want a life of my own? Is that too much to ask, Mother?"

"Now Ian, we've had this conversation countless times before, and I will not put up with your..." she began, but Ian didn't wait around to let her finish.

Instead, he promptly rose from his seat, and stalked out of the room.

"Ian, don't do this to me again." called out Lady Granville, but it was too late.

Ian stormed out of the living room, and marched up the grand staircase to his room, being sure to slam the door behind him. He was sick to death of this pampered life-style he had been brought up in. Why couldn't they just leave him alone? Then his thoughts drifted off to the girl he had rescued the night before. She was gorgeous. What he wouldn't give to see her again. But he knew he was chasing a pipe-dream. She had a man waiting at the car, she had said. And she probably wouldn't even remember him after last night. In dejection, Ian sat down on his bed, staring out his large picture window at the vast expanse of London. Storm clouds were rolling in across the Thames, and the rumble of thunder matched his mood perfectly.

Meanwhile, downstairs, the telephone rang loudly in the drawing room. Lady Granville leaned over and lifted the receiver.

"Lady Granville." she answered. "Ah, Natalie. It's so good to hear from you. Why, I was just about to tell my son that you were back from America. What's that, dear? Oh, of course. Legally you're not aloud to *live* in the estate yet, but there's no law saying you cannot hold a ball there. A masquerade? Oh how lovely, Natalie. It could be a coming home party of sorts. I'll be sure to invite all the large families I know. Of course dear. Alright. Goodbye." Lady Granville hung up the phone gently, her mind dizzy with excitement.

Just then Lord Granville strolled into the room.

"I say, you're looking terribly chipper, my dear. What's all the excitement about?" he asked.

"Oh, George, Natalie just called and said that she's planning a masquerade ball at the estate! She'd like us to be the hosts. It's going to be the event of the year. I think we should go all out on this. It's been years since anything like this has happened." babbled Lady Granville.

Lord Granville smiled, kissing his wife on the cheek.

"Whatever you think is best, darling. By the way, has our wayward son returned yet? I've been meaning to have a word with him." he replied.

Lady Granville sighed, seating herself.

"Our dear son is in one of his moods again. He saved a girl from being mugged last night, and now he's out to find this girl. Honestly, I don't think we can patch up these scandals for much longer." she complained.

"He'll be the death of me yet." sighed Lord Granville. "I'll try and talk to him. You just have fun planning this gala." he said, smiling reassuringly to his wife.

With that, Lord Granville left Lady Granville buzzing about excitedly, making all the preparations.

Elsewhere, Natalie hung up the phone in her room.

"I've just talked with Lady Granville. She said that she would be more than happy to help us put together a masquerade ball. Now all we have to do is get our costumes." Natalie chattered happily.

Grace was ecstatic. "Oh this is going to be marvelous! Handsome men decked out in dashing costumes and women with masks and fans, and lovely gowns..." she rambled.

Natalie looked at Elizabeth who returned her look. Then both girls took Grace's arm and pulled her towards the door.

"Come on, Cinderella. We've all got to get ready for the ball." Natalie teased. Grace laughed, grabbed her coat, and the three girls took off for the limo.

Once at the costume shops, the girls felt overwhelmed. There were racks upon racks of beautiful gowns just perfect for a masked ball. But with determination in their eyes, the girls set to work searching for the perfect gown. Natalie rummaged through costumes of Cleopatra, Marie Antoinette, Queen Elizabeth, Cinderella, Sleeping Beauty; but none seemed right. Suddenly, Grace's triumphant cry caught her attention.

"How's this girls?" she asked parading out in a flamboyant costume from the movie, *My Fair Lady*. "Wouldn't it be loverly?" she said, faking an English accent, leaning against the long, elegant parasol.

Natalie laughed. "It certainly is pretty, but how would you where a mask with that hat?" she pointed out.

Just then Elizabeth came stumbling out in a full length gown from *Beauty and the Beast*. Both Natalie and Grace gasped. It was the perfect dress for Elizabeth!

"Elizabeth, it's wonderful! Do you have a mask for it?" asked Natalie.

Elizabeth pulled a hand from behind her back revealing a gold, diamond encrusted mask attached to a thin gold rod.

"Of course." Elizabeth said, curtsying elegantly.

Natalie smiled, but Grace pouted.

"Why can't *I* find something like that?" she huffed.

But Elizabeth pointed behind her.

"There's a whole bunch more costumes back here." she said, leading Grace further into the shop.

Natalie barely even listened as Grace called off the costumes.

"Um, *Phantom of the Opera*, Snow White, Little Mermaid? I think not. Audrey Hepburn's *Breakfast at Tiffany's*, Grace Kelly, Scarlet O'Hara. Don't they have a princess category?" Grace chattered on.

Natalie ignored Grace and instead dug as far back into one of the closets, pulling out a lovely gown of solid white with ruffles all down the front and tiny jeweled sequins glinting in the light. And on the floor next to the dress were a pair of pearly white high heeled shoes. Natalie gasped in awe at the simple beauty of the costume. She glanced hastily at the tag. It read: Princess Diana. Just then, Grace popped her head over Natalie's shoulder.

"Oooh! I simply *must* have that dress. It's gorgeous!" she gushed.

Natalie sighed, but graciously handed over the gown to her cousin.

"Oh! It's divine!" Grace continued, squealing and disappearing into the nearest changing room.

Natalie rolled her eyes and went back to work searching for a dress for her own self. But in frustration, she sat down on the floor, looking terribly depressed. At that moment, the sales clerk walked by.

"Can I help you find something, Miss?" she asked sweetly.

Natalie looked up gratefully.

"Yes, *please*! I just can't seem to find the right costume for me. I'm having a masquerade ball, and I want to wear something elegant, but not too showy. But I just can't seem to find anything." Natalie sighed.

The sales clerk placed her fingers on her temples as if in deep concentration.

"Let me think here. I'm not sure if it's still here, but we used to have an absolutely stunning gown tucked away upstairs. It hasn't been used once, so it's practically brand new. Come with me." she instructed, leading Natalie up a set of creaky wooden stairs. Soon Natalie and the sales clerk had entered a dusty old room filled with antiquated costumes that seemed to be straight out of the 16$^{th}$ century. Natalie followed closely behind the woman as she pawed through the various gowns, clouding the air with puffs of dust. Moments later, after much digging and sneezing, the woman cried out in triumph.

"Aha! I've found it." she declared, pulling a dress off a nearby rack.

She quickly moved into the light, revealing the dress to Natalie. It was a beautiful dress of a silvery color, embedded with diamonds throughout. Its sleeves were long and made of lace, ending at the top of the wrists. And stitched on the back were a pair of lacey, almost transparent wings. She immediately recognized the costume from the movie *Ever After*.

"I guess it's supposed to be a butterfly, although I'm not particularly fond of the wings myself. I could remove them if you'd like." offered the woman.

But the more Natalie stared at the dress, the more she thought the wings added to the dress. It was perfect. She would wear an ornate pearl-white mask, covering only her eyes, adding the final touch to her costume.

"No. That's alright. I love it the way it is. How much will it cost to rent it?" Natalie asked, fingering the fabric in her hands.

The woman stood muttering and mumbling to herself, adding figures in her head.

"Well, if you want it for a week, it'll be about ten pounds. And every day after that is an extra fifteen. But, considering the fact that this dress hasn't been used at all, I could sell it to you for thirty pounds." the woman stated.

Natalie's eyes lit up.

"I'll take it!" she exclaimed, and rushed off to try it on.

Chapter 6

The evening of the masquerade ball had finally arrived. Lady Granville had insisted that Natalie not arrive until the party started, thus allowing her time to decorate the Ragion Estate. The servants had worked tirelessly all day long cleaning the old, stately mansion, and now the rooms were bright and spotlessly clean. There were fresh flowers in the conservatory, a fresh coat of paint for the drawing room, and all the lights had been polished thoroughly. Lady Granville was ecstatic. She had absolutely outdone herself. She quickly dashed into the dinning room where the servants were just beginning to light the candelabras.

"Is everything ready?" she asked, her voice bubbling with excitement.

The servants assured her that it was, just as the large grandfather clock struck 6:00 in the hall.

"Oh, it's time. They should be arriving at any minute now!" she chirped, and swiping an hors d'oeuvre from off a tray, she fled from the room to change into her costume.

Natalie sat fidgeting in her seat in the limo. Elizabeth sat on her left and Grace on her right. All three wore large sables over their costumes, not wanting anyone to see their costumes before the ball. But while Elizabeth and Grace talked over Natalie, Natalie sat twisting her gloves nervously. Finally, noticing her, Elizabeth asked,

"Natalie, what's the matter with you? If you keep that up, your gloves will be ruined!" she insisted.

But Natalie smiled vacantly.

"I'm not actually wearing these gloves with my costume, Elizabeth. Oh, I'm so nervous! I've never done anything like this before in my life." she said in a whisper, trying to catch the first glimpse of the Ragion Estate.

Grace and Elizabeth both took one of her hands.

"Nat, listen to me. I've known you your whole life. Believe me when I say, you're gonna be great." Grace said, squeezing Natalie's hand in hers reassuringly.

Just then, John pulled the limo into the Ragion Estate Gate. The three girls craned their heads against the window for a better look. The house was enormous! It was at least five stories tall, with big marble stairs that came down to the drive where one unloaded from one's car. Already there were hundreds of cars, lined up as people entered the house. Natalie became flushed with excitement.

"You guys, we're actually going to do this!" she squealed.

All three girls hugged and squealed together as John pulled up in front of the mansion. And as the servant opened the door, the squealing ceased immediately, and three well-poised girls emerged with their heads in the air. But unfortunately for them, while they had their heads held high, they missed the first step, tripping and bumping their shins. The servants quickly helped them to their feet, as all three blushed deep crimson.

"So much for poise!" hissed Elizabeth to her friends.

They thanked the servants for their assistance, and climbed daintily up the stairs and into the large hall.

Once through the massive doors, all three girls gasped in awe. The room they had entered was enormous, and filled with elegantly dressed people adorned in fabulous costumes. The hall stretched on with several doors on either side. In the center of the hall ceiling hung an ornate crystal chandelier that glistened brightly. Upon their entering, a servant came, bowed and took the girls' wraps and gloves. Next to them stood a man in what looked like a page-boy's costume.

"What name shall I give?" he asked politely.

"Name?" the girls asked puzzled.

"What name shall I use to announce for you?" he explained.

"Oh, um...Miss Natalie Ragion of Devonshire, and her two friends, Elizabeth Lancewood of Harrison, and Grace Vanclick of Houghton Lake." Natalie stated.

The man nodded, turned to the throng of people and in a loud voice announced, "Presenting Miss Natalie Ragion of Devonshire, Miss Elizabeth Lancewood of Harrison, and Miss Grace Vanclick of Houghton Lake."

All eyes seemed to turn towards them as cameras flashed at the three girls who smiled, curtsied, and waved. Grace was eating this up as she posed for each camera dramatically. The other two laughed, eventually pulling her away.

Suddenly, Natalie heard Lady Granville's shrill voice.

"Natalie!" she called out loudly, rushing through the throng of guests.

Natalie smiled at the sweet older woman, while Elizabeth and Grace looked on in shock.

"That's the rich Lady Granville?" asked Grace in disbelief.

Natalie nodded her head, chuckling.

"Yep. And she thinks I'm her *'adorable'*, rich niece." Natalie replied.

"I thought she would be more...poised." Elizabeth mused, as Lady Granville sprinted (or rather wobbled) across the hall.

Natalie laughed, as she placed her ornate mask over her face.

"You may have a chance yet, Nat. If *that* woman can make it in high society, so can you." Grace whispered.

Natalie shushed Grace, just as Lady Granville approached.

"Oh my dear, how lovely you look. These must be your young American friends." Lady Granville bubbled. "I'm Lady Granville, which I'm sure you already knew." she said, extending her gloved hand.

Grace took the hand and curtsied slightly.

"I'm Grace...Vanclick. Natalie and I have been going to school together for years." she introduced.

"And I'm Elizabeth Lancewood, another friend." Elizabeth said modestly.

Lady Granville smiled broadly.

"It's so nice to meet both of you. Now, Elizabeth and Grace, the punch and hors d'oeuvres are at the end of the hall, and the dancing is in the ballroom. But if I may, I'd like to steal Miss Natalie away." she said, gently taking Natalie's arm.

"Of course. Thank you, Lady Granville." Grace called back, as Natalie and Lady Granville disappeared into the crowd.

"I do believe we're on our own, Grace." laughed Elizabeth.

"What does it matter? As long as Natalie's identity is safe, I don't care who I'm with at this party." Grace said, elegantly taking the side of her dress in one hand and descending the stairs.

"Excuse me, ladies…" interrupted a deep voice from behind.

Grace and Elizabeth spun around in surprise only to come face to face with Natalie's bodyguards.

"Oh my gosh!" gasped Elizabeth in surprise. "You…you scared me, er, us, that is." Elizabeth stammered out nervously.

James Butler bowed stiffly, trying to hide his grin from Elizabeth.

"Sorry about that. I was just wondering…*we* were just wondering where Miss Ragion was?" he asked.

Grace pretended not to be interested, but found her eyes constantly wandering back to Michael Masterly.

"I thought she gave you the night off?" Grace said, staring vacantly at her gloves. At that, Masterly slapped his forehead as if remembering.

"Oh, yes. That's right. It *must* have slipped our minds. Looks like we made a trip here for nothing, eh James?" said Michael quickly.

James shook his head, and after a curt nod, turned on his heels to go. But before they could leave, Elizabeth shot Grace a quick look and the two girls spoke up.

"Um, now that you're here..." Elizabeth began.

"...you simply must have the punch. It's exquisite!" Grace gushed. Then, realizing her mistake, she quickly added, "Not that I've tried the punch, but I'm sure if I did that it would be exquisite."

Michael let out a loud laugh, breaking the ice between them. Grace blushed deep crimson, but soon found herself laughing as well.

"Shall we?" asked James, extending his arm to Elizabeth.

Elizabeth smiled up sweetly at the man, and linked her arm in his, heading off down the stairs.

"How about we try that punch?" suggested Michael to Grace.

Grace nodded, curtseying lightly, and the two followed Elizabeth and James down the stairs.

Meanwhile, Natalie had met just about enough of the upper crust of society to last her a life time. She had been shaking hands, receiving hugs, and getting her hand kissed by just about everyone in the room!

"Now the one person I *really* want you to meet is my son. Although, I just can't see why he's late. I'll go and see what's keeping him. You just wait right here, my dear." insisted Lady Granville, shoving her way through the crowds.

Natalie let out a sigh. How many more people would she have to fool into thinking she was the poor little rich girl? Despite Lady Granville's request, Natalie slipped off into a side room that appeared empty, and shut the door quickly and quietly. Natalie then spotted a long sofa with its back to the door. In relief, Natalie rushed over to it. She attempted to jump over the back of the couch, but only managed to make it half way. She sat precariously perched on the back of the couch, with her gown snared at the base. Natalie fidgeted with her dress when all of a sudden; the snare came loose, sending Natalie tumbling backwards onto the couch! In one swift motion Natalie wound up lying on her back with her feet dangling over the back of the couch, and her head hanging off the cushions of the couch. Natalie let out a sigh.

"Why me? What have I done?" she muttered to herself.

Suddenly, to her dismay, Natalie heard the door open and close quickly. Natalie held her breath as footsteps sounded on the tiled floor. Someone was in the room. Just then, she heard the voice of one of the servants speaking to someone else.

"Sir, your mother is quite concerned as to your whereabouts. Shall I inform her as to your arrival?" asked the servant.

"Absolutely not!" replied a frantic male voice. "My mother is trying to set me up with a girl. No, I'm happy in here." continued the voice.

From the sounds of it, Natalie assumed the owner of the voice to be a younger man.

"Very well, sir." sighed the servant, and the door opened and closed once more. Frantically, Natalie tried to pull her feet over the couch, but instead only managed to fall loudly off the couch all together!

"Oof!" she groaned loudly as she landed on her back, her costume wings fanned out beneath her.

Suddenly, the sound of footsteps came rushing towards her. Natalie held her breath in apprehension.

"Hello there." said a voice above Natalie's head, "Just hatched from your cocoon, have you, Madame Butterfly?" he joked.

Natalie craned her neck to see the speaker, and replied.

"I say, what's the idea of sneaking up on a poor girl?" she demanded.

The speaker was a tall man of about twenty or so, and had thick brown hair. His face was obscured by a Harlequin mask, and only his deep blue eyes stared back at Natalie. His costume was a royal blue suit with black riding pants and knee high black leather boots. On his shoulders, he wore epaulettes of gold, giving him the look of an English soldier.

"I'm sorry, Miss. I thought I was alone in this room." he said, helping her to her feet.

Natalie laughed nervously.

"So did I." she retorted. "I really don't make it a habit of lying on the floor at parties, but my dress got caught, and I couldn't seem to get free." Natalie said, trying to explain her unusual predicament.

The man laughed a light, clear laugh. It seemed to Natalie that she had heard that laugh before.

"It's alright. I thought at first you might have had some bad punch, and were in here trying to sleep it off. But I see I was wrong." he stated.

Natalie smiled at him, an awkward silence filling the room. Just then, the man paused and stared strangely at Natalie.

"Um, exactly how much of that conversation did you overhear?" he asked quickly.

Natalie smiled, wiping a strand of her hair out of her face before answering.

"Just the part where you said you were hiding from your match-maker mother." teased Natalie.

The young man shook his head and laughed.

"I was afraid of that. It's just that my mother has this tendency to try and set me up with any female that breathes. No matter their weight, height, or stature." explained the man.

Natalie laughed at the man's predicament, thinking of her own awkward situation with Lady Granville trying to set her up with *her* son.

"I know the feeling. Actually, I came in here to hide from my date too." Natalie replied, peering through a crack in the door.

"Oh, you have a date?" asked the man, a tinge of disappointment in his voice.

But Natalie quickly shook her head. Just then she saw Lady Granville looking around the room perplexed. Natalie had to smile to herself at her own cunning.

"No. But if I'm not careful, I will. There's a woman out there who wants to set me up with her son. Problem is, I haven't seen her son in ages, so I don't really want to be forced into that kind of a situation." Natalie said, sitting in a chair next to the door.

"Yeah, that doesn't sound too fun." said the young man also taking a peek out of the door.

Just then, he noticed Natalie bouncing her feet to the tune of the waltz playing in the ballroom.

"Hey, what if you and I were to be each other's date for the evening? We wouldn't even have to tell each other our names if we didn't want to." suggested the young man extending his gloved hand to Natalie.

Natalie thought it over, and quickly decided by accepting the man's hand.

"Agreed. We'll each be a mystery date." answered Natalie cheerfully. And with that, the young man led Natalie out onto the dance floor.

# Chapter 7

Together, Natalie and her mystery partner swept out into the swirling masses dancing the various waltzes being played. Natalie was thoroughly enjoying herself. At first she had been afraid that she'd have to dance with a bunch of "old family friends" and be bored out of her head. But instead, here she was being swept away by a mysterious stranger who treated her just like an equal, rather than like the spoiled heiress that she was portraying.

As the two swept across the ballroom, Natalie couldn't help the feeling that she had seen this mysterious stranger before. But she couldn't think of where.

"Are you sure we haven't met before?" Natalie asked at length. "You seem very familiar to me." she added thoughtfully.

"Uh oh. I hope you're not asking me to take off my mask. Cause I think we agreed not to." he laughed.

"Yes, but you can see three quarters of my face, and all I can see are your eyes. Now how is that fair?" insisted Natalie playfully.

"Well, how do you know that I don't *need* this mask?" challenged the young man, his eyes staring deeply into Natalie's.

"Oh, please. Next you're going to tell me that you wear that mask to hide your scarred visage." joked Natalie.

But suddenly, the man stopped dancing and stared hard at Natalie.

"H...how did you know that?" he asked in a serious tone.

Suddenly, Natalie felt terribly nervous and ashamed for having just blurted out such an insult.

"Oh...I'm so sorry. I had no idea. I just..." she stammered, placing a hand to her mouth in alarm.

But suddenly the man burst out laughing.

"Hey, I was just kidding. Relax. I promise you that my face isn't scarred." he answered, laughing.

"Ugh! You're terrible." she laughed, slapping his arm. "You made me feel horrible for saying anything. Thanks a lot!" she pouted, her eyes looking teasingly into his.

"Well, if it makes you feel better, I'll reveal my identity before the night is over. Maybe just before we leave. How would that be?" challenged the man.

But Natalie just laughed. She was enjoying herself far too much to care what the man's name was. She just wished that the evening would continue like this forever.

"It's good to see Miss Ragion enjoying herself." Michael Masterly said in his mellow quiet voice. Grace turned her head and caught sight of Natalie in the arms of a mysterious handsome stranger smiling into his eyes like a love-struck school girl.

"Tell me about it. Would you believe she actually didn't think she could pull this off? I mean how hard is it to *pretend* to be a socialite?" Grace chattered, not realizing what she was saying. Michael cocked his head to one side curiously.

"What do you mean by that?"

"OH! Just that...you know...she hasn't..." Grace stammered nervously, "she doesn't remember much about

English society, so she's been pretending that she remembers it all. It's slowly coming back to her though." she added quickly.

"Ah. I see." Michael replied, obviously not caring about what she had said, but rather staring into Grace's eyes, mesmerized. Grace stared back all too eagerly.

"See what?" she asked, not really hearing what he had said.

"Nothing." he smiled, "I was just watching your face."

Grace gasped suddenly, "What's wrong with my face?" Her fingers flew to her cheeks, feeling them carefully.

Michael chuckled and pulled a strand of Grace's brown hair away from her face. "Absolutely nothing." he assured her. Grace smiled up at the man, letting the music of the waltz carry the two of them across the ball room floor.

The evening was a smashing success. Lady Granville couldn't have been happier at the turnout. Everybody that should be, was there. She smiled to herself as she spotted Natalie in the middle of the room, entwined in a slow dance with her son Ian. The two of them were smiling at each other fondly. She couldn't have planned this reunion better. Just then, she became aware of someone behind her.

"Really, Gwendolyn you've outdone yourself." cooed Lady Deuhurst, smiling cattily.

"Ah, Madeline. How nice you look tonight. So glad you and your husband could join us for the celebration. I just want to let you know that I think it terribly sweet of you to have taken Natalie under your wing like you did. I hadn't realized how hard it would be for her to re-enter British society after so many years, but I see that with your help she's doing splendid." chattered Lady Granville, fanning herself rapidly. Lady Deuhurst merely nodded her head in politeness, hiding a sneer behind her elegant fan.

"It was nothing, really. I'm just happy to see her so happy after all this time. Such an unfortunate turn of events with her parent's accident, then being shipped off to America. I suppose it's the mother in me that's taken such a fondness for her." she gushed.

"That's sweet to hear. I don't mind admitting, Madeline, that at the time of the Ragion's death, I rather didn't like you and your husband." Lady Granville admitted timidly. Lady Deuhurst feigned a shocked expression as Lady Granville continued, "I know I shouldn't have, but I thought of you both as more interested in the inheritance and who received what than the fate of the daughter. I know now that I couldn't be more mistaken. It's so good to have people like you in our circle of friends." she insisted, patting Lady Deuhurst's arm affectionately. "Well, must run, dear. So many people to see. You know how it is." she laughed, bustling off into the crowds.

"What was that all about?" came her husband's voice from behind her. Lady Deuhurst turned and slipped her arm in her husband's, smiling slyly.

"The old bat was just clearing her conscience to me. Telling me how glad she is that we're all 'friends' now. Just you wait and see how friendly I can be once we've exposed her ridiculous mistake."

At that same time, James Butler had been standing just behind the corner where the Deuhursts stood and overheard the entire conversation. Just then, Elizabeth came over smiling happily.

"Your drink, my lady." offered Butler, handing her a glass of punch.

"Well, thank you sir. You are truly a gentleman." she teased, as the two of them strolled around the room. But even as they walked, James kept his eyes fixed on the Deuhursts, pondering what he had heard.

"So how did you end up as a bodyguard, James?" Elizabeth asked, breaking into his line of thought. He smiled, laughing sheepishly.

"Well, to tell you the truth, this was supposed to be just a temporary position. Don't get me wrong, it's a great job and I get paid well, but it's definitely not what I hope to make a career out of. I graduated from Cambridge with a degree in language studies. I had hoped to teach French, but when money got tight; I called on some old family connections and managed to land this job. Perhaps someday, when the opportunity arises, I'll get the chance to be a language teacher. Perhaps even travel to another country and teach French there." he explained. Elizabeth smiled, clearly impressed at James' ambition.

"That sounds fascinating. Maybe one day you could teach in America." suggested Elizabeth, finding a secluded seat in a corner. "Have you ever been?"

"To America? Not yet. Although, I'd love to go sometime." he replied, but a shadow seemed to cross his face, "Will...will you be staying on here with Natalie, or will you be heading back to the US soon?"

Elizabeth reeled from the question. She had totally forgotten that they had all been living this fairytale with no thought of the future! Eventually, they would all *have* to go home. Yet the thought of leaving, weighed heavily on her heart.

"Um, I'm actually not sure. You know, there's just so many things going on right now that I hadn't given it much thought." she quickly replied, "Has anyone ever told you that you look a lot like the actor Bradley Cooper?" Elizabeth asked randomly, desperately hoping to change the subject. James laughed loudly.

"I dare say you're the first to ever compare me to him." he smiled. James finished off the last of his punch, rose from his seat and took Elizabeth's hand. "Come on. It's almost twelve, and I want at least one more dance with you." he insisted. Elizabeth was only too happy to be twirled out into the mass of couples swaying to and fro on the dance floor.

"Crisis averted." she thought, staring into his ocean blue eyes. "Or, at least momentarily."

As the large grandfather clock in the hall chimed twelve, Lord and Lady Granville made their way to the foot of the grand staircase. Lord Granville motioned to the orchestra to stop playing as the crowd hushed.

"I want to thank all of you for being here tonight at Miss Ragion's homecoming ball. It's so nice to be able to see old friends, and even nicer that they're wearing masks to hide their age." The crowd laughed politely.

Grace arched an eyebrow. "That was supposed to be funny?" she whispered loudly. Elizabeth elbowed her sharply in the ribs, silencing her immediately. Grace rubbed at her side and shifted closer to Michael so as to avoid further abuse, and turned her attention back to Lord Granville who was still droning on.

"And so, let us please make welcome back to England, our very own Miss Natalie Ragion." he concluded. The crowd burst forth in applause as Natalie pressed through the crowds and made her way up the steps. Lady Granville hugged her tightly, kissing her loudly on the cheek. Natalie's eyes instantly scanned the room for her mystery date, but to her dismay, he seemed to have vanished!

"Just my luck." thought Natalie, bitterly. That was two men in less than a week. So much for her prophetic dream on the plane. She quickly brought her attention back to the crowd of people applauding her.

"Hi. Hello. Thank you all." Natalie waved awkwardly, feeling terribly nervous, "It's so nice to be back...here. At my...home. You've all made me feel so welcome, and I can't thank you enough for all your support. So, have an enjoyable evening, and..." she stammered for some way to wrap up her impromptu speech, "Enjoy...the food?" she added questionably. The crowd looked slightly confused as they resumed their applause.

The orchestra resumed its music and the crowds swept back out onto the ballroom floor. Natalie descended the stairs, escorted onto the floor by Lord Granville with Lady Granville at his side.

"You must indulge an old sentimentalist with at least one dance, Natalie." insisted Lord Granville.

Natalie smiled, "Of course Uncle George. I'd love to." Natalie floated off into a waltz with Lord Granville, gracefully following his lead.

"I think your arrival back was just about perfectly timed. You could be of great use to my wife and me." Lord Granville stated. Natalie looked confused.

"Use? How so?"

"Our son, Ian. He's something of a troubled child, I must confess. You were very young when you knew him last. Fourteen, was it?"

"Yes, I think that's about right." Natalie said hesitantly.

"Well, he's something of a problem in the social limelight. Nothing legal of course, but just a constant need to be disruptive. He loathes our social status. You may have read of the embarrassing scandal last summer when he tried hitchhiking across Europe dressed in rags. We caught him, before he got very far. When we asked him why he had done it, he said he wanted to live life." explained Lord Granville somberly.

Natalie listened intently. Even though she didn't know this 'Ian' he sounded like someone she could sympathize with. After all, wasn't it her own attempt at "living life" that had gotten her into this mess? Perhaps, she and Ian had more in common with each other than she thought.

"And now?" Natalie asked.

"Well, his last year at school has been fairly quiet so far as we know. But since he's been back, he's already returned to his usual antics."

"Uncle George, how do you think I'll be able to help?" asked Natalie incredulously.

"Well, you can keep him occupied. After all, you're the one person that's affected him the most. I don't think he ever got over it when your parents sent you to America." Lord Granville seemed desperate. "Just do your best to try and use the friendship the two of you have and point him in the right direction. I know as a parent, that's supposed to be our job, but at this point in life, Ian isn't really keen on listening to us. So I'm of the mind that he may listen to an old childhood sweetheart, just returned from abroad. Please, darling, for Gwendolyn and I, please?" he urged.

Natalie sighed and smiled. "I promise you, I'll do my best. But I doubt he'll even remember me." stated Natalie as Lord Granville chuckled.

After several minutes, the waltz came to a close. Lord Granville bowed politely, as Natalie curtsied in response. Natalie desperately wanted to find her mystery partner before the night was over, and before someone else insisted that she dance with them. Suddenly, Natalie felt something, a paper, pushed into her palm amidst the pressing crowds. She hastily glanced around for the messenger, but no one out of the ordinary caught her attention. She carefully stole a glance at the hand-written note.

*Meet me on the second-floor balcony. You promised that we'd unmask ourselves by midnight.*

"Excuse me, Miss Ragion?" a voice spoke behind her. Natalie spun to face Lord Deuhurst in a crisp, black suit and bow-tie, no mask. He looked like the villain from some old movie. All that was missing was a bowler hat and pencil moustache. "May I have the pleasure?" he asked, extending his white gloved hand. Natalie crumpled the note and tucked it beneath the edge of her sleeve at her wrist. Reluctantly, she took Lord Deuhurst's hand and joined into the next dance. Unfortunately for her, it was a slow dance. Natalie seemed to see the clock hands moving much too slowly. Lord Deuhurst pulled Natalie strangely closer to him as he leaned his head towards her ear.

"A rousing speech, my dear. So…heartfelt." he said in a low tone. Natalie glanced up nervously. Was he joking or serious?

"Lord Deuhurst, I'm not…" stammered Natalie, "I'm just trying to get this over with. The sooner the *real* Natalie returns, the better for me." she insisted, avoiding the cold stare from Deuhurst.

"Relax, my dear Miss Rashion. Even now my people are locating her. You have but to keep up pretenses a bit longer, then we'll seamlessly pull a switch and no one will be the wiser." he explained. Natalie sighed in relief. "But I caution you. Don't get too comfortable with your role. It *is* temporary.

I know the glamour of wealth and high society can be dazzling and alluring." he added.

Natalie stopped dancing, "I assure you, Lord Deuhurst, I have no desire to collect on that inheritance." she stated boldly. "This is simply a case of mistaken identity."

Lord Deuhurst smiled, "Of course. And it will soon be remedied. Enjoy the remainder of your evening, my dear." he bowed curtly.

Natalie gathered up her skirt and flew from the room. She pushed past the crowds, pausing at the foot of the grand staircase to make sure that no one was watching, and ascended the stairs away from all the prying eyes. Once on the second floor landing, Natalie strolled along the ornate hall towards two French glass doors that lead out onto a marble balcony. The cool night air seemed to wash over Natalie as she stepped out onto the balcony overlooking the expansive manicured lawns. Directly below was the gravel wrap-around drive lined with limousines. Beyond that was a gorgeous stone water fountain lit up with rose tinted lights, coloring the jets of water as they sprayed upward. The lawn itself was boxed in by perfectly trimmed hedges as tall as a lamp post.

"It's beautiful, isn't it?" a voice interrupted her reverie.

Natalie gasped in alarm, but smiled as she turned to see her mystery date half sitting on the edge of the railing. "It is." she simply agreed. The man walked over to Natalie's side, leaning his elbows against the marble railing and staring out over the estate. Silence seemed to fall between them.

"I enjoyed your speech." the man chuckled. Natalie immediately flushed deep red.

"Where were you? I looked but you weren't there. How could you have heard my speech?" demanded Natalie.

"I have my ways," he replied, then added, "Natalie." Natalie smiled sheepishly. "I hadn't realized that I had been dancing with the guest of honor all night."

"Well, then perhaps you should have been a bit nicer?" she laughed. The man continued to smile at her, his eyes locked with hers. "I know those eyes." her voice was a whisper as his face seemed to lean in closer. The next thing Natalie knew, she was kissing him! Or he was kissing her. She wasn't quite sure. It was all so sudden. And exciting, and terribly frightening all at once. He pulled away, grinning as he pulled off his Harlequin mask, revealing the very same man who had saved her from the mugger on the bridge!

"Hi. I'm Ian." he stated simply, moving in for another kiss. But Natalie stepped back in shock.

"You mean to tell me..." she began, "You're the guy...the mugger, the no-name. My *date* for the evening?" Natalie was horrified. The very man she'd been hoping to see again was, in fact, the son of Lord and Lady Granville, and the man she had admitted to have been avoiding.

"What? Are you disappointed? Mad? Happy? Bewildered? I'm having a little trouble placing your mood right now." Ian asked quickly.

Natalie shook her head, "I think it's all of the above. Disappointed because I've made a fool of myself tonight in front of you. Mad, because you let me do it. Happy because, well I *really* wanted to find that guy from the bridge again. And bewildered, because you and I were originally supposed to have been reintroduced by your mother tonight, and somehow we ended up together anyways." Natalie said, exasperated.

Ian laughed, "I agree. That is a lot going on all at once. And then, the whole kiss thing didn't make things any easier. Sorry, I guess I'm a bit impulsive, you could say."

"Have to agree with you there." muttered Natalie.

"Let's try this again. Miss Natalie Ragion, allow me to officially introduce myself. I'm Ian Granville, heir to the Granville estate, average college student, all around lazy chap, and yet eager to get to know you more." he stated grandly. Natalie couldn't help but smile. She had to admit, this guy had charm.

"It's nice to make your acquaintance, Mr. Granville. Again, that is. And I very much look forward to getting to know you better as well." she laughed, holding her hand out. He gently took it and kissed it softly.

"I look forward to it."

# Chapter 8

Weary and worn out, but terribly happy, the trio of friends tumbled into their room at 3:00 in the morning. Grace fell unceremoniously onto her bed with a loud "Oof." While Natalie seemed to be sleepwalking/staggering around the room, dropping a glove here, her sable in a heap there, and stepping out of a shoe over here. Elizabeth yawned loudly, bending over only to bump heads with Natalie.

"Ow! Watch it." she moaned in a slurred voice.

"Sorry, Nat." Elizabeth muttered, heading off to change for bed.

"Where were you guys all night? I didn't see you once." Natalie said, unclipping her hair.

"I was dancing. Michael is a great dancer." Grace garbled, her face buried in her pillow, muffling her voice. She sluggishly lifted her head, "What about you? Who was your mystery man tonight?"

Natalie smiled to herself before answering, "Ian Granville."

"What? You mean you actually spent the entire evening with the guy Lady Granville was trying to set you up with?" Elizabeth exclaimed, coming from the bathroom.

"Yeah. And wow, he's amazing! He's so…" she let her sentence trail off, searching for the perfect superlative to describe him.

"Ok. Yeah, we get it. Very nice. Very cute, I'm sure." Grace replied, pulling the blankets of her bed over her head. "It's late. We can swap boy stories in the morning." she insisted. The others agreed and soon were all fast asleep.

The next morning, the three girls chattered eagerly about their dates the night before. Natalie found it funny that both her friends had fallen for the two bodyguards, but she was pleased that it worked out so well. This way, wherever she went, the girls had an escort.

"So, I saw you dancing with Lord Deuhurst towards the end of the night. What was that about?" Elizabeth asked, sipping her tea.

Natalie made a face, "I don't know why, but that guy gives me the creeps. He wanted to make sure that I wasn't planning on actually signing the inheritance papers. I mean really, I think by then they'd probably catch on that I'm not who I say I am." she replied.

"Which begs the question, how do you plan on telling everyone when the time comes?" Elizabeth asked tentatively.

"I really don't know. The Deuhursts keep telling me that for the good of everyone, I should just keep up the charade for now, but now I've got the Granville's to worry about, their son, Ian; John the limo driver, Michael and James, my bodyguards. It's all getting so twisted." Natalie sighed, and placed her head in her hands.

"I think you need a break. Come on. Today, we're going sightseeing. Just the three of us." Grace insisted. Natalie smiled and allowed herself to be lead away to change.

Donning some of her own clothes, as opposed to the ritzy style of her doppelganger, Natalie wore a pink polo shirt, some denim capri's, and a pair of white sandals, for which her feet were grateful. She tossed her hair into a ponytail, grabbed a handbag and was ready to go. Grace and Elizabeth dressed similarly, so as to avoid the stress of pretending to be a socialite for one day. As Natalie opened the door to the hotel room and stepped into the hall, she gasped in surprise. Standing idly by, was her two bodyguards. But very different. James looked like a typical college student in his t-shirt and jeans, while Michael looked to be ready for a game of tennis in a crisp white polo shirt with khakis.

"Um…hi guys. What's with the outfits?" Natalie asked skeptically. She had to admit she was a little annoyed. Today, she was supposed to just be normal Natalie Rashion. It was her one chance to see London as a tourist, and not a source of gossip.

"We…um…may have texted them and told them about today." admitted Grace coyly.

"Don't be mad, Nat. They're more here for us than you." insisted Elizabeth, squeezing Natalie's arm playfully. Natalie sighed then smiled.

"Oh alright. Fine. But you two better not act super protective and all that. Unless I'm obviously being attacked, I don't want to know that you're my bodyguards today." ordered Natalie, tossing her ponytail over her shoulder.

"Absolutely." agreed James, linking arms with Elizabeth, and Michael followed suite with Grace.

But as they emerged from the elevators, Natalie spotted the mob of journalists waiting just outside the hotel lobby, eager for a shot at the rich new heiress.

"You've got to be kidding me." moaned Natalie.

"We could try the kitchen?" suggested James, pointing to the double doors beyond the front desk.

"You think they'll let us?"

"One way to find out," whispered Michael, taking Grace's hand in his and slipping between the doors. The girls giggled and soon the group was making a mad dash through the crowded kitchen, passing wide-eyed chefs and busboys, hurriedly stepping aside. Finally, they found a small exit that lead to an alleyway behind the hotel. The girls stumbled out laughing, and trying to catch their breath.

"Alright, that has to be the best exit ever. I'm going to remember this the next time I leave the hotel." laughed Natalie.

"I'm sure you're not the first celebrity to use it either." Michael added. "The press can tend to be a bit much when it comes to a new celebrity in town."

Soon, the group was casually strolling along the busy streets of London. Natalie breathed in the atmosphere. This is what she had wanted. To be part of the throngs of people going about their everyday lives. Elizabeth eagerly snapped pictures as she went. They visited the Parliament Building, took pictures of Big Ben, made their way to Westminster Abbey, and stopped just outside the Tower of London.

"You know it's a wonder were not all three locked up in there right now." whispered Elizabeth to Grace and Natalie while James and Michael went to get ice cream from a vendor. All three girls stood leaning on an iron fence running around the Tower.

"That's for sure. If the Deuhursts don't find Natalie soon, we're going to be a regular trio of jailbirds." moaned Natalie.

Suddenly, someone grabbed at Natalie's wrist, causing her to scream in alarm. Instantly, without looking, Elizabeth and Grace began pummeling the attacker with their purses and kicking his shins and knees viciously. The attacker kept protesting, trying to shout something, but the screaming of the girls drowned out anything he was saying. It wasn't until

Natalie took a step back that she realized that her "attacker" was in fact Ian!

"Oh my gosh! Ian?" she called out. Almost immediately, Elizabeth and Grace halted their onslaught, their purses in mid swing. Ian smiled, smoothing his clothes and attempting to stand up straight. But at that instant, James and Michael came barreling down, roughly tackling Ian to the ground.

After several minutes, and much explaining and apologizing on both sides, Ian brushed himself off.

"Yikes. That's a mean couple of friends you've got there." he grinned, rubbing at his sore legs. "I'm just lucky none of you lot had any mace."

"Who in their right mind would use a mace nowadays? I use pepper spray." Grace declared haughtily. She still wasn't too impressed with Mr. Ian Granville. Ian stared at her blankly.

Natalie grinned, trying to suppress her laughter as Elizabeth leaned over to Grace and whispered, "Um, Grace? Mace *is* pepper spray."

Grace looked confused. "I thought a mace was that big medieval weapon. You know that ball with spikes on the end." she explained. She paused for a moment, "Oh wait." she said, realization setting in. Ian laughed heartily.

"Now I'm *really* glad you didn't have one of those in your purse." he joked. Despite herself, Grace couldn't help joining in the laughter.

"So we're you following us?" Natalie asked, as the group continued their London stroll.

"Maybe." he said slyly. "I was actually on my way to see you, but that mob at the front of the hotel blocked my way. When I finally managed to get through, I learned from the concierge that a group of five had recently made a hasty kitchen escape. From there, it was easy to follow you. I only just caught up when your friends decided to mob me." he explained. "So what's up with all the cloak-and-dagger? You out for a day of sightseeing?" he asked.

Natalie smiled nervously, "Well, you know. It's just been so long since I've been able to walk around London, so I figured I'd ditch the heiress, and trot out the tourist."

Ian smiled, "I know what that's like. Or have you already forgotten our little rendezvous at the bridge?"

"Oh, believe me. That's one night that'll be hard to forget." she laughed. Ian smiled a knowing smile, before Natalie quickly interjected, "Well...you know...because I almost got mugged, and stuff."

Ian's face fell. "Oh great. I see that I left no lasting impression on you whatsoever."

"Sorry. It's not that. I...this is just...this is very new for me." Natalie admitted, walking along side Ian.

"What? Relationships or getting mugged?"

Natalie smirked, arching an eyebrow, "Very funny." Then she turned serious, "But both, to be terribly honest." she admitted, fidgeting with a flower she had snatched from a nearby fence. "Everything lately has been like a dream. I mean, the inheritance, meeting and trying to get to know everyone," she explained, "Then, there's you." she paused.

"Oh come on. You mean to tell me that the elegant young heiress hasn't had at least a dozen suitors until now?" he asked skeptically. Natalie shook her head. "Not even one? Even while in America?" he pressed.

"Nope. Not one. This is brand new territory for me." she said, avoiding eye contact. She demurely placed her hands behind her back, head down, walking slowly. Ian grew serious.

"Wow. I guess I just assumed that since you were, you know, a socialite and everything, you'd have guys lined up around the block. You know, turning heads, breaking hearts."

Natalie looked incredulously at Ian, "Well thanks for that. It's always flattering to know how others see you." she quipped sarcastically, walking ahead of Ian. He rushed up next to her grabbing her arm and turned her to face him.

"No! That's not what…I didn't mean it like that. It's just, you're so…refined. I figured it would come easy to someone like you. I mean, it took me all of about ten seconds of that mugging that night on the bridge for you to leave an impression on *me*." he stated quickly. Natalie paused, smiling slightly. She rolled her eyes.

"Refined? Yeah that's me. I was so refined when you found me tripping over myself at the ball. Hey everybody, come meet the refined young heiress falling over the sofa and hiding in the study." Natalie joked. Ian laughed, linking his fingers in hers and kissing her hand.

"You were…you *are* beautiful, Natalie. And I'm sorry if I'm moving fast. Like I said, I'm impulsive. But I promise to rein it in. We'll go slowly. Who knows where this is going." he said softly.

"Let's take it slow and enjoy the ride." agreed Natalie.

Just then Grace came rushing up with Michael, her face flushed and worried.

"Good grief, you two! What's taking you so long? Michael and James want to take us on the London Eye. Hurry it up." she urged, arching an eyebrow at Natalie. Natalie just smiled, nodded and followed along with Ian at her side.

Riding on the London Eye was fantastic. It provided the girls a spectacular view of the London skyline. The girls took countless pictures, until finally the men succeeded in dragging them away. From there, the ensemble made their way to the broad expanse of Hyde Park where they lounged on the rich green grass, soaking up the sunshine. They bought lunch from some street vendors, idly feeding the ducks with the leftovers.

"Oh man, this is the life. I could live like this forever." sighed Grace, lying with her hair fanned out on the ground around her.

"That begs the question; will you two be staying on with Natalie once she inherits the Ragion Estate?" Ian asked.

Grace sat up very suddenly, realizing her mistake. Natalie shot her an evil glare. She silently mouthed the words, "Nice going."

"Um…that depends. You know…there are our families to consider. I mean we can't very well just call home and be all 'Hey there mum and dad, I'll be moving to England at the end of the summer. Cheerio! Toodle-pip, and all that.'" she stated in a heavy British accent. James Butler laughed.

"You do realize we don't all talk like that, right?" he asked. Elizabeth grinned.

"Apparently in Grace's mind, anyone who's remotely British still speaks like their from the Victorian period." she teased. Grace threw a wad of her sandwich at Elizabeth which prompted a small flock of ducks waiting nearby to charge Elizabeth, resulting in a short bout of shrieks and laughter and much quacking.

As the afternoon drew to a close, the sun's dying rays drew long shadows along the vast green park, creating a quiet, cool atmosphere.

"I've got a great idea." Ian piped up. "Why don't the six of us all head down to my parents' summer home in the country this weekend. It'll be just us six, and it will give all of us a chance to get away from the mobs of nosy reporters and such." Ian suggested.

The group readily agreed that it would be great to get away for a bit, with the added bonus of seeing the English countryside. So it was agreed that early that Friday morning, Natalie and the girls, accompanied by the bodyguards, would meet up with Ian at his parents' home several hours outside of London.

"Perhaps once were there, someone can finally teach you how to *really* play croquet." laughed Elizabeth. Natalie laughed before hushing Lizzie. Then she thought how the weekend couldn't come fast enough.

Chapter 9

Friday dawned bright and sunny as the girls all tumbled into the waiting limousine, packed and ready for the country. While Lizzie and Grace chattered away with Michael and James, Natalie dreamily watched the London scenery go by. Soon, the towering buildings were replaced by rolling green hills and a distant view of the ocean. They passed by quaint little towns that looked to have been plucked right out of a storybook. Overhead, the sky was a cerulean blue, dotted with tufts of wispy white clouds. Listening to her friends, Natalie had to laugh at how much her two bodyguards had changed since she had met them. She was glad to see that they were just as equally love-struck by her friends, as her friends were of them. She tried not to think of what would happen when this charade ended.

Eventually, the road they were on turned off into a small, one-lane, dirt road. The narrow lane was shadowed overhead by a long row of willow trees that hung down forming a sort of tunnel, with slits of sunlight peeking through. After a mile or so, the lane opened up into a broad lot where, off to the right, sat a quaint, two story cottage. Its white washed walls were contrasted by dark blue shutters, and from the red-brick chimney, a swirl of smoke could be seen. There was a vast wrap-around porch with a pathway leading down a grassy hill to a pond just beyond the trees. The entire place seemed hedged in by the forest surrounding it. It looked perfectly peaceful.

"Wow! I think this house is bigger than my parent's back home." gasped Elizabeth, stepping out of the vehicle.

"Yeah, I think mine too." whispered Natalie, standing in awe.

Grace took a step forward, taking in the house. "Ah, the rich sure do know how to live." she stated grandly, marching up the pathway to the house. Elizabeth and Natalie laughed, following behind as James, Michael, and John brought up the luggage.

As they marched up towards the porch, Ian stepped out smiling broadly and spreading his arms to gesture at the land around them.

"Welcome, everyone, to Serenity's Pond." he greeted.

"Serenity? Sounds like someone's name from a soap opera." Lizzie laughed.

"Yeah, but who in their right mind names someone 'Serenity'? I mean for a house, yeah, but for a person?" Natalie giggled.

Grace furrowed her brow, turning to look at Natalie and Lizzie. "That's another thing I love about the English. They get to name their houses. That's *so* cool!" she declared.

Michael laughed, "Actually, it's typically only the nobility and upper class that do that, Grace. We 'commoners' don't often give our homes names." he explained.

"If I named my home, it'd be something sophisticated like, the House of Lake Houghton." Grace stated dramatically. "How about you, Lizzie?"

"Um, probably something like Lizzie's house."

James snickered as Grace huffed in indignation.

"Ugh. As per usual, Lizzie, the ever-practical one."

Natalie swept past the girls and their guys, into the warm embrace of Ian. She smiled up into his eyes.

"Hi." she simply stated.

"Hi, yourself. Took you lot long enough. I've been waiting here for hours." he replied, hugging her tightly. "James, Michael, don't worry about the bags. The house staff will see to it. Right now, we've got a date with the stables." he called, leading Natalie around the porch.

"Stables? That's it. I'm in heaven." sighed Grace.

At the back of the cottage stood a neatly-kept riding stable. Natalie inhaled deeply as she stepped into the shady building. Instantly, she began coughing and snorting. Her nostrils were assaulted by the strong stench of hay, horses, and other such smells associated with livestock.

Soon, the entire group had selected a horse and was following Ian and Natalie's lead through a scenic pathway through the woods. Each of the couples made sure to give the others some distance. Lizzie struggled to get her horse to move in a forward direction as her horse seemed intent on taking a more scenic route through the underbrush. She squealed as the horse meandered through thistles and low hanging branches. James tried not to laugh as he diligently tried to guide both his horse and hers back to the main path.

"Of course I'd get the one horse who doesn't want to follow the path." she complained, relentlessly clicking her tongue at the stubborn animal.

"Lizzie, what *are* you doing?" Grace called as she and Michael trotted past them. "Don't you remember anything of how to ride? We used to do it almost every year with Natalie for her birthday, remember?" she laughed.

"We were also like twelve years old and on a set path. This horse just doesn't like me." she yelped as her horse paraded through a thicket of brambles. Grace laughed as she and Michael cantered off together, leaving a struggling Lizzie and an amused James behind.

Meanwhile, up ahead, Ian turned and watched, smiling, as Natalie gazed in awe at the beauty around them.

"Do you like it?" Ian asked at length.

Natalie turned to him and smiled sweetly. "Its perfect, Ian. I love it. Thank you for sharing this with us."

"You're welcome." he smiled back.

"I can't believe how beautiful it is out here. It's like... something from a Jane Austin novel."

"You act as if you've never seen the English countryside before. Surely, this pales in comparison to the places your parents used to take you." Ian replied. Natalie turned her eyes downward.

"Well, I don't really remember much about my childhood with my parents. I guess being away has made it all kind of hazy." she stated slowly.

"Well, do you remember us as children?" Ian inquired.

"Not really." she laughed. "Why? What do you remember?"

"I remember this really annoying little girl who couldn't stand me following her around, tormenting her." Ian told her. She laughed in response as he continued. "I especially remember this particular summer, where your parents and mine spent the entire summer at one of your parents' summer homes near the beaches of Dover. You were about thirteen years old, and I was fourteen. I remember you and me building sand castles and burying each other in the sand. We spent almost every day out there." he recalled, seeming to stare off into another time.

"Wow. You really remember all the details." Natalie replied.

"Well, why wouldn't I? That's where I got my very first kiss." he paused, staring intently into Natalie's eyes. She felt the blood rush to her face, the heat spreading all the way up to her ears which started burning in embarrassment.

"Ian...I..." Natalie began, but Ian cocked his head in confusion.

"You mean, you really don't remember that?" he asked, puzzled and slightly hurt.

"I'm sorry, I don't." she replied curtly, spurring her horse into a trot, putting distance between Ian and herself.

Natalie pushed the horse on faster and faster trying to outrun something she couldn't explain. Here she was listening to this poor, incredibly sweet guy (Ok, maybe *not* so poor) recall this amazingly sweet memory, and she just sits there listening and lying to him? She felt guilt creep over her like some foul disease. She felt horrible. It wasn't until she felt the hot, stinging tears rolling down her face that she realized she had come to a halt at the edge of the pond, her self-loathing and frustration pouring out. Her horse nickered lightly, shaking its thick white mane, and continued its grazing. How long must this go on, she thought despairingly. What had started out as a silly, frivolous adventure was turning into a tangled web of lies and deceit. Suddenly, she felt a hand touch her arm gently. She frantically wiped at her tears, turning to face Ian.

"Natalie...I'm sorry. I didn't mean to..." he began, clearly confused. But Natalie shook her head instead.

"Oh no, Ian. I'm sorry. Here you are recalling such a beautiful memory and I..." she wanted to blurt out the truth so badly. "Ian, I'm not..." she began, but a lump seemed to form in her throat, stopping her. But even as she tried to take deep breaths to clear her thoughts, Ian leaned over from his horse and tenderly placed both his hands on Natalie's face and softly kissed her.

"You don't have to be sorry about anything, Natalie." he whispered. She smiled weakly, and leaned over and hugged Ian tightly. The thoughts of her confession seemed to slip away as she reveled in this beautiful moment in time.

*******

The following day dawned bright and sunny yet again. The birds sang loudly outside the girls' bedroom window, alerting them to the start of another day. Elizabeth yawned loudly, rolling over in the large bed that all three girls were sharing.

"Uhnnnnnnn. BequietI'mtryingtosleep." mumbled Grace, barely coherent.

"You guys, I think I want to be a photographer." Elizabeth stated, sitting up suddenly. Her tangled hair stuck out at odd random angles all over her head.

"And what prompted this morning revelation?" Grace asked, rubbing sleepily at her eyes.

"Well, you know when this is all done and everything, I'm going to try and get James to come to the States, and get a job teaching. He could teach French while I pursue a career in photography." she declared happily.

"Wait a minute. What do you mean, 'When this is all done'?" asked Grace, suddenly wide awake and sitting up.

"Lizzie, you didn't tell him, did you?" she asked aghast. Lizzie playfully pushed Grace back down onto the bed.

"Of course not, you dork. I'm just saying that I know this can't go on forever. And I *really* like James, and he seems to like me too. So I'm just making preparations for the future." she explained.

Grace sighed, "I guess you're right." she took a deep breath, exhaling slowly.

"What? What's wrong with you?" Elizabeth asked.

"I was just thinking about Nat. I've been figuring, and there's no way this is gonna end well. No matter which way you slice it, someone ends up getting hurt. And it's either gonna be Ian or her. Or most probably, both."

"Well, maybe he'll understand and be okay with it." suggested Elizabeth, carefully trying to smooth her wild hair.

"Yeah, and maybe the man in the moon will come down and give us some of the cheese that the moon's made of. And then we'd have a picnic with Big Foot, and…" she scoffed.

"Ok, ok. You made your point with the man in the moon. No need to go on."

"Lizzie, come on. Seriously, what would *you* say if the guy you liked suddenly said one day, 'Oh by the way, I'm not really who I say I am. Still wanna be friends'?" she quipped. "I never thought I'd be the one to say this, but I'm sorry we ever even started this in the first place. I mean, don't get me wrong. This has been one of the most fantastic summers of my life, but I hate to think of what's going to happen." she explained. Lizzie nodded in agreement.

"I know. I mean, when did this whole thing get so complicated."

"Um...by the way, where *is* our rich young heiress?" Grace suddenly asked, glancing around at Natalie's empty side of the bed.

Natalie closed her eyes as the warm morning sun seemed to wash over her. She smiled to herself as the sound of the water lapping gently against the side of the row boat seemed to rock her in a gentle rhythm. She had woken up at the break of dawn, something she almost never did voluntarily, and had headed down to the pond for a quiet morning walk. Unexpectedly, she had run into Ian who was doing a bit of morning fishing. Judging by the tangled state of his fishing line, and the loud grunts and mumbling, she assumed he was having a bad time of it. But at the sight of her, he rowed to shore and offered to take her for a ride around the pond.

"A penny for your thoughts?" Ian's voice broke into her reverie. Natalie opened one eye, squinting in the bright sun.

"I thought that was an American expression." she laughed. Ian smiled as he rowed the boat closer to the center of the pond. Natalie was reclined at the front of the little rowboat while Ian masterfully maneuvered it around the quiet pond.

"Just because the yanks invented it doesn't mean we Brits can't use it too. Now, what were you thinking of?" he persisted.

Natalie sighed. "I was thinking how I wish this weekend could go on forever." she said dreamily.

"Yes, but then it wouldn't make it very special, now would it? Besides, I know I'd get sick of this place pretty quick."

"Well, that's easy for you to say. You and your parents own it. You can come here anytime you want."

"Oh come on, Natalie. You've got like a million different places like these that you could go. With your name and your inheritance, you could vacation just about anywhere."

Natalie paused, sitting up and wrapping her arms around her legs as she rested her chin on her knees. "That's not what I meant, though. I want *this*. Right here, right now. This very moment. The quiet, the solitude, the warm sun." she hesitated, "With you…here." Her face flushed a little as she stared into Ian's deep blue eyes.

"I'd like nothing better." Ian placed his hand on hers, holding it for a moment.

"What would you do if you had no title?" Natalie asked abruptly. Ian laughed, taken aback.

"What do you mean?"

"I mean, if you weren't born to privilege, what do you think your life would be like?"

"To be honest, I've never really given it that much thought. I mean, sure, I've thought how it would be nice not to be bogged down with my title and the airy, frivolous social class, but I've never actually thought about it in depth." he replied. "What about you?"

Natalie smiled, "I think I would be an adventuress. I would love to travel to different countries, especially with my friends. Life would be simple. I'd have a family that loved me. I'd have grown up in a white, two-story house with a dog or two just outside the city. I would definitely have siblings. Of course I'd end up going to college, but not until I'd traveled a bit. You know different parts of Europe. I'd make it a point to go to Ireland. There's something fascinating about that country. But most importantly, I'd just be happy being me." A silence stole over the two as Natalie inadvertently described her *actual* life to Ian.

"Wow." he replied softly. Natalie turned her attention back to the present.

"What?"

"It's just...you. You have your dreams so intricately laid out. So much detail."

Natalie laughed nervously, "So, how about you?"

"Well, I'll be the first to admit, if I could just leave my title behind, I'd travel abroad. I'd go to America and see all the big name cities. Particularly New York. I mean, I realize London is great, but there's just something about New York that fascinates me. And during this whole time, I'd do what I love best." he said.

"And what's that?"

"I'd become a writer." he replied simply.

"A writer? I had no idea. Have you written anything?"

"Well, sort of. I've tried my hand a few times, but I can never seem to finish anything." But at this, his face seemed to cloud over.

"What's wrong?"

"Nothing. I guess, all this talk about wishing things the way I want them. It makes me realize how terribly trapped I am. My whole life is planned out for me." he explained bitterly. "I'll continue my education at the academy. Probably learn something like law or business. Then, return to London and to my parents where my father will put me in charge of some dull charity foundation or wealthy corporation or another and whenever he grows old and tires, he'll pass the title of Lord Granville on to me. This of course includes the endless parties, the social events, and the stuffy decaying aristocracy that my family heritage is so well known for." he declared caustically.

A cloud seemed to drift in front of the morning sun, temporarily creating a shadow over the pond. Natalie felt a chill run through her as she let a silence fall between Ian and herself. She didn't know how to respond to this. They were opposites. He was of the upper class, and she of the lower. He was trapped by his wealth, and she was beneath him because of it. These situations were always complicated.

"I'm sorry about that. I didn't mean to go off and vent like that." apologized Ian, running his hands through his hair. He smiled sheepishly.

"Ian, you have every right to vent. I'm only glad to listen. But there's something we both should remember. We are slaves to our obligations. Life gives us responsibilities, and like it or not, sometimes that's just the way things are. Believe me, there are so many things I wish I could change. But in the end, I have to submit to the way of things, and comply." she reminded him. He smiled as he took both her hands in his. She leaned closer towards him, rocking the boat slightly.

"Natalie, ever since you've come back…you make everything seem like it'll turn out all right. And I know that with you in my life, I'll happily face any obligations I have to." he vowed. Natalie once again felt the burning pangs of guilt roiling inside her. She wanted so badly to tell him the truth.

"GOOD MORNING YOU TWO!" Grace shouted loudly from the dock. Natalie jumped in surprise, abruptly standing to her feet in the boat. But her sudden movement rocked the boat awkwardly, tipping her to one side. With a loud splash, Natalie fell headlong into the pond. Grace shrieked, cupping her hands over her mouth as Ian laughed and tried to fish Natalie out. But instead, Natalie resurfaced, spewing water and laughing.

"Are you alright, Nat?" Grace called out.

"I'm fine, Grace. The water actually feels great." she called back. "I'll meet you at the dock, Ian." she insisted, floating on her back as she back-stroked towards the nearby dock. The water felt warm as the sun beamed down on her.

As Ian tied off the boat, Grace gave Natalie a helping hand and pulled her from the water. Natalie attempted to ring out her hair just as Grace cocked her head in confusion, staring at Natalie.

"What? Do I have algae on me?"

"Nat, what are those things?" Grace asked curiously pointing at something on Natalie's neck. Grace reached out a hesitant hand and touched the 'thing' on Natalie's neck. It squirmed in response.

"EEEEEEEEEK!" she screamed in terror, recoiling her hand instantaneously.

"What? What is it?" Natalie shrieked, trying to feel what Grace had touched. But as she brought her hand up, she saw it. Leeches! About twenty leeches had attached themselves to Natalie's arms, legs and neck. In a frenzy, Natalie began hopping up and down, waving her arms like a maniac, screaming for help in removing the leeches while Grace screamed in chorus, running in mindless circles around the dock, too freaked out to do anything. Ian tried his best to keep from laughing at the two frantic girls as he grabbed Natalie and quickly ushered her back up to the house, followed by a paranoid Grace who was checking her own skin for signs of the nasty little beasts. As they entered the house, the others came running, alerted by the high-pitched hysterics.

"Someone get me something to remove these leeches." Ian instructed.

"Should we start a fire?" Grace squealed, still waving her arms. Ian looked incredulously at her.

"For what?"

"I don't know. Doesn't heat make leeches let go?" she asked anxiously.

"Well, unless you plan on torching your friend like Joan of Arc, I don't recommend that." he quipped.

"I've got it!" Lizzie's voice echoed from the other room. She came charging into the living room with a large salt shaker and instantly began dousing Natalie with salt.

"What are you…" Natalie began spitting the salt out of her mouth as it hit her face, "…doing, Lizzie?" she asked bewildered. But within moments, the salt had done the trick and a nasty pile of shriveled up leeches were being swept up as Natalie left to go shower and change.

Meanwhile, Lizzie and Michael had managed to calm the frenzied Grace who was now sipping coffee in the kitchen, still checking herself for leeches every now and then.

"Ugh! I can't get those nasty little creatures out of my head. I feel like my skins crawling." she shuddered.

"Oh it's not your skin. Its that leech right there." Lizzie joked pointing towards Grace's arm. The reaction was instantaneous as Grace leapt from the chair, swatted at her arm, shrieking, and ran from the room. Lizzie couldn't help but laugh.

"Oh that was too easy." she sighed.

The phone rang loudly, breaking into the moment. Upon answering it, Lizzie was greeted by Lord Granville.

"I hope you kids are having a grand time out there."

"We can't thank you enough, sir. It's absolutely gorgeous out here."

"If it's not too much trouble, would you mind putting Natalie on the line? I've got some urgent business with her."

Elizabeth called for Natalie, handing the phone off to her, heading off in search of Grace to further torment her.

"Hello Uncle George. How are you?" Natalie greeted cheerily.

"Well, I'm alright my dear, but I'm afraid I've got some rather important news. All the paperwork for your parent's estate has arrived and it's going to need to be signed by this next week. Now, don't you worry though, because I've already set everything up. This Tuesday we'll hold a press conference at your parents' estate where you and I will sign the papers. It'll be a nice photo opportunity for you as well. Sort of a public way of letting society know that you've inherited everything legally." he explained. Natalie felt her legs grow weak, sinking into a kitchen chair.

"That sounds...great." she said half-heartedly. "You've thought of everything. Thank you. I'll see you and Aunt Gwendolyn this Tuesday then. Goodbye." she hung up the phone, staring blankly at the wall. So it was time. The dreaded moment had arrived. The moment the charade blew up in her face, crossing the lines of 'honest mistake' and into 'legally wrong.' There was no way that she could, in good conscience, sign the papers entitling her to a fortune that wasn't even remotely hers to begin with. Natalie felt the panic building.

Just then Grace came rushing into the room with an irritated look on her face.

"Elizabeth, if you don't get that slug away from me, I will personally throw you into the pond!" she declared vehemently.

"Oh come on. It's not a slug, it's a snail." she laughed, cradling it in her hand.

"Slug, snail; same thing. Snails are just slugs with backpacks!" she huffed. But as both girls glanced over at Natalie sitting vacantly in the corner, they immediately stopped their discussion.

"Nat, are you okay?" Lizzie asked tentatively.

"I'm dead." she replied simply.

"Um...not to contradict you, but you look pretty alive to me." Grace said, hoping to take the edge off. But Natalie just shook her head.

"Its over. This whole...*thing*, whatever you want to call it. It's done. I cannot and *will* not be a part of this anymore." she confessed.

"What? What is it that's happened?" Lizzie inquired.

"Lord Granville just called and told me that everything is in place for me to sign the Ragion Estate papers this Tuesday. He's even holding a press conference." she groaned exasperatedly, holding her head in her hands.

"Oh that's bad." Grace admitted.

"You think?" Natalie snapped.

"Well, we all know how the last press conference turned out. Maybe we could write a speech in advance." Grace continued.

"I think you're still missing the big picture here, Grace. I am **not** Natalie Ragion! I am a nobody from Michigan who's been lying and deceiving everyone including myself since the moment I got here. And now, its time to face my mistakes head on. I will simply have to tell them the truth." she blurted out.

"What? The truth? No, not the truth. That'll only make it worse. The truth means an ugly scene, lots of harsh words, prison, and then possibly beheading!" Grace insisted.

"Actually, I have to agree with Grace." Lizzie spoke up, "I mean, not about the beheading thing. That's just weird. But perhaps before we go and blow the lid off of this, why don't we check in with the Deuhursts and let them know about the situation. Maybe they've been able to finally locate the real Natalie by now."

Natalie nodded her head, "Alright. Yes. Good plan. I'll call them first." she stated, picking up the phone and dialing.

"Let me know what's up. I'll be out on the patio with James." called Lizzie, heading out.

Once on the porch, Lizzie settled into a lawn chair next to James who sat peacefully soaking in the sun.

"What's all the commotion inside?" he asked lazily.

"Oh its nothing. Just a bit of drama. Natalie's on the phone with the Deuhursts right now, so I decided to come and keep my favorite bodyguard company." she smiled sweetly. James suddenly became alert.

"The Deuhursts? What's Natalie's relation with them anyway?" he asked cautiously.

"Well, they've just taken an interest in her since she arrived. They've been very helpful. Why? Don't you like them?"

"Oh, it's not about me. It's just something I heard at the ball. Lady Deuhurst seems very...vindictive. I get the feeling she's trying to wheedle her way into Natalie's circle for her own benefit." he explained.

"Hmmm. Well, she's seemed very nice to all of us. If she's got an ulterior motive, I certainly can't see what it is." Lizzie replied simply.

Meanwhile, Natalie was frantic as she relayed the story to Lord Deuhurst. She blurted out the situation, and begged him to find a solution.

"Please my dear, just remain calm. This situation is entirely under control." his smooth, steady voice encouraged her. "In fact, I've got the real Natalie Ragion en route to London as we speak. It seems she missed her flight for another bound for the Caribbean."

"But what'll we do? Won't they realize that we're two different people?" Natalie asked anxiously.

"Well, here's the catch with that one. I will assume full responsibility, and just simply explain that you were posing as Miss Ragion for security reasons, and that you were in fact hired as her double back in the states. I will be sure to gloss things over, and everything will be forgiven, I assure you. Just trust me." he implored.

Natalie sighed, "If you think it'll work, I'm willing to try it. I'll just be glad when this whole thing is over."

"Won't we all, my dear. Won't we all." Lord Deuhurst chuckled. Natalie *really* didn't like the sound of his laugh. It sounded smarmy and snake-like.

As she hung up the phone, Grace, who sat eagerly next to her, looked expectantly at her.

"So? What's up? Good news?"

"Yes." Natalie heaved a sigh of relief, "Lord Deuhurst has a way to make it seem like I've been hired as Natalie Ragion's safety double. He'll explain everything to the crowd on Tuesday." she explained. She massaged the sides of her temple gingerly. "This whole thing will *finally* be over."

Grace leaned back in her chair, "Yes, but what does that mean for you?" she asked quietly, but pointedly.

"What do you mean?"

"Well, from the looks of it, a certain young man seems entirely infatuated with 'Miss Natalie Ragion of Devonshire' and I happen to know for a fact that my cousin, Miss Natalie Rashion of Roscommon is also head over heels for him. What are you going to do about that?"

"The only thing I can do. Tell him the truth. He deserves to know." she said resolutely.

"Well, if you think it'll work. But personally, I'd wait till this little weekend trip is over. It wouldn't do to drop a bomb like that on him in the middle of vacation." admonished Grace.

"Oh Grace, what happens if he hates me? I really like this guy, and yet everything we've shared has been built on a lie."

Grace leaned over and hugged her cousin tightly. "Don't worry, Nat. This thing will turn out right in the end. Just you wait and see. Remember, I'm the romantic. I know these things." she smiled. Natalie laughed and sighed. Hopefully, she was right.

# **Chapter 10**

The trip home was both sweet and sad for Natalie. She loved the time spent at Serenity's Pond, and hated having to say goodbye. She knew that a difficult time lay in store for her as Tuesday marched ever closer. The limousine dropped Ian off at the Granville estate and returned the girls to the Grand London Hotel on Monday evening. Natalie had slipped Ian a note before leaving the car insisting that he meet her before the press conference. She pleaded with him in the note that there was something she had to tell him before anything else happened.

"Well, tomorrow's the big day." Grace said somberly. "Do we really have to attend the signing?"

"I don't think we'll actually be there for the signing. We'll meet the Deuhursts before hand, and after I talk to Ian, we'll slip out before the press spots us. Lord Deuhurst will make the announcement without me being there. The last thing I want is to face a crowd of people that I've lied to while the cameras and journalists assault me for answers. That can only end in chaos." Natalie explained.

"Well, this being your last outing, I still think you should go in style. It'll be the last time you get to dress up on the rich Natalie's dime, so I suggest you take advantage of it." Grace insisted.

"Then I leave that up to you, Grace. I'm feeling a bit tired. I'll see you guys in the morning." Natalie said softly. She slipped silently from the room under the watchful eye of Lizzie, while Grace eagerly returned to her position as fashion consultant for one last occasion.

Elsewhere, Ian seemed to be bouncing off the walls with eagerness and rapture. He came barreling into the sitting room, startling Lady Granville severely.

"Good gracious, Ian! What's gotten into you? You sound like a herd of cattle tramping through the house like this." she gasped, setting her tea cup down. Ian laughed and swept over to his mother and took her hands in his, pulling her from her seat and began waltzing with her around the room

"You look lovely tonight, mother. Absolutely stunning, really." he rambled. Lady Granville giggled, but pulled away from her son.

"Alright. What strange spirit has possessed my son?" she asked mockingly, fanning herself from the excitement.

"Natalie has. She has bewitched me, mother. I've never met anyone quite like her. She's so...beautiful. Yet unassuming. Unlike any other debutante I've ever seen in our circle of society. She's so ordinary, yet exciting. She challenges me to think, to dream, to feel alive. She's amazing!" he effused, stalking about the room excitedly. Lady Granville smiled broadly.

"Ian this is wonderful! She's just the sort of girl your father and I had hoped you'd meet." she assured him. Ian rushed to the side of his mother's chair where she sat and knelt down.

"Mother, I'm in love with her." he stated matter-of-factly. "In fact, I'm so in love that I can't seem to imagine life without her. Now I'm sure you and father will think this rushed, but right after the conference on Tuesday, I'm going to tell her how I feel, and give her this." he exclaimed, producing a small black jewelry box.

"Um...Ian darling. That may be just a tad bit hasty. I know you're impetuous, but darling this is all so hurried. Real love ought to take time. It's built and worked on through the relationship. Not thrown together in a day or two. That's just infatuation, you're talking about." Lady Granville tried to caution, but Ian would have none of it. Instead, he kissed his mother chastely on the forehead, and leapt to his feet.

"Call it what you will, Mother, but I know what I'm feeling." he called as he dashed from the room.

"Good heavens. The boy is mad." Lady Granville whispered.

The following morning was a typical London day; overcast and pouring rain. The fog could be seen rolling in off the Thames and seemed to cover the city in a dreary, chilly blanket of gray. Natalie woke first and after reminding herself of the day, prepared to get ready. Grace had set out for her a simple red dress. After putting it on, Natalie checked herself over in the mirror. The dress had no sleeves and came just above the knee. She had paired it with simple red heels and a small red clutch with black trim. Natalie pulled her hair up and pinned it fashionably. As she finished preparing, the girls awoke and stumbled into the large bathroom.

"Oh very nice, Nat." Lizzie gushed, taking in the outfit.

"Thanks. And thank you, Grace. Its perfect." she replied. Grace smiled and arched an eyebrow.

"Can I pick 'em, or can I pick 'em?"

Natalie seemed in a daze as she and the girls prepared for the day's events. She barely took notice of her breakfast, staring idly out at the rain and fog as the raindrops trickled down the balcony windows.

"Hello? Natalie, did you hear me?" Lizzie's voice interrupted.

"What? Oh, sorry Liz. I guess I was daydreaming." she apologized; sipping her coffee only to find it had gone cold.

"I was asking that since this whole thing is up today, would you mind if I told James the truth? I really want to try and convince him to come back to the States with us."

"Oh yeah, sure. But if you could, let me talk to Ian first. I don't want to have to deal with anything until he knows the truth." she pleaded. The girls agreed, and Natalie returned to her daze.

All too soon, the knock came at their door as John entered in his crisp chauffer's uniform.

"Ready to go, ladies?" he smiled.

Natalie felt her heart beat faster as her palms began to sweat. She was so terribly nervous. Not about what people would say, but how Ian would react. She couldn't believe how strong her feelings were towards him after such a short time. But sometimes, these things happened like that. You don't plan to fall in love. It just happens. And Natalie knew now that she was indeed in love. What else could explain the anxiety, the excitement, and the giddiness building up inside her? How could she explain this pain she felt at possibly losing Ian? She cleared her throat and held her head high.

"Yes, thank you, John. We're ready to go." she announced clearly. The girls followed behind as Natalie lead the way from the room.

Out in the hall, James and Michael assumed their positions on either side of her, marching to the elevator. Once inside, Natalie squeezed both Lizzie and Grace's hand for assurance. Both girls squeezed back and assured her that everything would be fine. She took several deep breaths. The elevator bell dinged, and the doors parted. Show time. She walked with a confident air about her as she crossed the hotel foyer. Out in the pouring rain, the mob of journalists and paparazzi were huddled beneath their umbrellas hoping for a glimpse of the young heiress. James and Michael propped open the double glass doors as John opened a large umbrella for Natalie and the girls, ushering them quickly into the waiting car. The only noise was that of the clamoring crowd and the pouring rain. But Natalie ignored them all, focusing on one thing; Ian.

The drive through the city seemed interminably long. Grace and Lizzie tried to make idle chatter, but Natalie barely noticed. Instead she noticed how the beat of her heart seemed to match the rapid whipping of the windshield wipers. All of a sudden, the vast iron gates of the Ragion Estate rolled into view as John eased the car up the drive. Already there were rows of cars lining up. Natalie gulped hard. She turned to the girls.

"Once we're inside, I need you to help me find Ian. Above all else, I need to speak with Ian. I'm supposed to meet Lord Deuhurst in the study, so if you find Ian before me, send him there." Natalie instructed. Lizzie took Natalie's hand in hers.

"Natalie, it's going to be fine. Don't worry. Soon, it'll all be over." she assured her. Natalie hugged them both.

"You guys are the best."

The car pulled up to the marble steps, and Grace swung open the door. She picked up the umbrella, and without thinking popped it open. Unfortunately, she forgot to make sure it was outside the car. The umbrella burst open, sending water droplets everywhere and cramping the already tight space.

"Smooth move, Grace." Lizzie muttered, scrunched into a corner trying to avoid the wet instrument.

Natalie laughed and with Grace's help, they managed to push the umbrella outside. Natalie rushed up the steps, her bodyguards behind her. She entered the grand hall, now seemingly so empty as compared to the night of the ball. The butler approached stiffly.

"Good day, Miss. Lord Granville is preparing for you in the ballroom, and Lord Deuhurst has asked that you meet him and Lady Deuhurst in the study."

"Thank you. Tell Lord Granville I'll be along directly." she replied, heading off for the study.

James and Michael followed close behind as Grace and Elizabeth slipped off in search of Ian. They first thought to try looking in the ballroom, but as they stepped in, the throng of cameramen, journalists, and socialites overwhelmed them.

"Yikes! Let's not go in there right now. I'd rather not fight that crowd, especially when they realize our charade." Grace whispered, pulling Lizzie by the arm from the room.

Instead, they took to the stairs, making their way along the myriad of halls and rooms.

"Good grief! There's like a million different rooms in this place. How are we supposed to know where Ian might be?" complained Elizabeth, opening another door.

"Natalie?" a woman's voice came from inside. Elizabeth and Grace poked their heads round the door where they saw Lady Deuhurst seated next to someone they didn't recognize. Upon seeing the girls, Lady Deuhurst whispered something to the stranger and sent her from the room through an opposite door.

"Come in girls, come in." she gestured to them.

"Sorry to interrupt. We were just looking for Ian Granville. Have you seen him?" Elizabeth asked.

"Why no, dears. I haven't. What do you need him for?" she asked sweetly. Almost too sweetly, Lizzie thought.

"Oh Natalie's looking for him. She needs to talk to him." Grace explained. Lady Deuhurst's eyes seemed to narrow.

"I can only imagine what she might need to tell him." she said sarcastically. Elizabeth was suddenly reminded of what James had told her before about Lady Deuhurst's vindictive attitude. She didn't like the evil look she was giving the girls, and she began to tug at Grace's arm.

"Oh, she needs to explain about the misunderstanding. You know the whole mix up thing." Grace prattled on, completely unaware of the change in attitude of Lady Deuhurst.

"I'm sure she does. Unfortunately, the time for talk and explanations is past, and I really must be going." Lady Deuhurst said suddenly, rising from the sofa.

"What do you mean by that?" Elizabeth challenged, intrigued by the change in demeanor.

"I mean that your dear friend Natalie has played the part of the patsy all too well. We can't have her running her mouth right before our big moment now, can we?" she asked, seizing both girls firmly by the arms and directing them to the sofa. "Have a seat, dears." she said in her disturbingly sweet voice.

"What? How dare you?" shouted Grace, aghast at what she had heard.

Lady Deuhurst blocked the door with her large frame, her brow furrowed, eyes menacing.

"You've been using us all along!" accused Elizabeth, jumping to her feet.

"But you were too stupid to realize it until now." sneered Lady Deuhurst. "But I'm afraid time's running short. I'll be back to let you both out after the announcement. Be back in a bit, my dears." she chuckled, slipping through the door. Lizzie and Grace charged for the door, but the resounding click of the lock assured them that they were trapped. They rushed for the other door, but it too had been locked from the other side.

"Well this is just great!" huffed Grace, slumping down into the sofa. "We didn't even see this coming."

"This whole time, they've been assuring us that they'd explain everything, and now they're probably going to pin this whole thing on Natalie!" exclaimed Lizzie angrily.

"But why? What do they hope to gain?"

"I don't know, but whatever it is, Natalie's in trouble and we've got to help her." insisted Elizabeth, pacing the room.

"It's hopeless, Liz. We're trapped in here. The conference is starting in five minutes. Unless you know how to pick locks, we're stuck." grumbled Grace.

Downstairs, Natalie was waiting impatiently for Lord Deuhurst in the study. She walked around the ornate room nervously, anxiously glancing up at the clock. She had been waiting for the past fifteen minutes, and still hadn't seen any sign of Lord or Lady Deuhurst. Just then, the sound of applause could be heard through the door leading to the next room. Natalie cracked open the door and peered into the adjoining room; the ballroom. It was packed with people, all awaiting her triumphant entry. She spotted Lord Granville at the front of the room standing behind a broad wooden desk littered with papers atop a small platform with a microphone nearby. He was speaking to the crowd, but she was far too anxious to hear what he was saying. That's when she spotted Ian. He was towards the front of the crowd next to his mother. He looked so incredibly happy. His face was practically glowing. Natalie sighed. She had to face her mistakes. It was the only way to make up for lying to everyone. Lord Deuhurst or not, she would simply march out there and explain her situation.

Perhaps things really would turn out all right, and everyone *would* understand and forgive her. Particularly Ian.

She heaved a big sigh, quickly smoothing her dress over. Then, with a resolute mind, she marched through the door just as Lord Granville gestured towards her direction. The camera flash-bulbs popped in her face, dazzling her with their bright lights. The low murmur of the crowd seemed to drone on as she walked up the aisle to the front of the room. She tried to plaster a pleasant look to her face, but she knew it wasn't convincing. She tried not to catch Ian's eyes, but inevitably, she did. His intense blue eyes seemed puzzled by her morose demeanor. She gave him a half-hearted smile, intending to continue past him, but his hand found hers and stopped her momentarily. As she turned back towards him, the din of the crowd seemed to swell as the cameras attacked again with renewed vigor at the sight of the lovely young heiress and her possible suitor.

"Hey, I tried to find you earlier, but you weren't in here." he whispered quickly. Natalie nodded and tried to pull away, but Ian held fast. "Are you alright, Natalie?" his voice urgent and concerned. She lowered her eyes, swallowing hard.

"Yes, Ian. I'm sorry. I tried to meet you earlier, but I was waiting to meet with someone. Look, Ian, whatever happens..." she began, her eyes pleading, but just then Lord Granville's jovial voice broke through over the microphone.

"Now don't monopolize the young lady, Ian. You'll see plenty of her afterwards." he laughed good-naturedly. The crowd chuckled in response as Ian smiled and Natalie blushed in embarrassment. She quickly slid her hand from Ian's, turning for the platform.

"I'll talk to you after?" he asked. Natalie turned to face Ian with a look of longing and pain. She mouthed the words "I hope so." as she made for the front.

Lady Granville smiled broadly at Natalie as she neared the edge of the stage. With a light squeak that Natalie could only assume was a sound of absolute happiness, Lady Granville reached out and hugged her tightly.

"This is it, my dear. Your moment." she gushed, slipping her some note cards. Natalie glanced down seeing some speech prompts thoughtfully written down for her. Perhaps word of her last speech had reached Lady Granville. Still, it was the thought that counted.

"Thank you, Aunt Gwendolyn." Natalie whispered, hugging back.

Lord Granville offered his hand as Natalie stepped up onto the platform, smiling politely and waving absently to the crowd. There had to be at least 200 people in the room. Almost every major news publication and several local television stations were represented. Their cameras, microphones, and recorders all pointed and poised at Natalie.

"On behalf of the late Neville and Luciana Ragion, I'd just like to take a moment and thank you for coming on behalf of their dear daughter, Natalie. It had been our pleasure to be friends of such a loving couple, and to now be reunited with their daughter makes this moment one to remember." Lord Granville began as Natalie stood awkwardly to the side, fidgeting with the folds in her skirt. "So without further ado, may I present the Lady Natalie Ragion."

The crowd erupted into applause as Natalie absorbed in the title she had just heard. It was the first time Lord Granville had actually used her inherited title, and it just made her even more resolved to end this ridiculous façade. Taking a deep breath, Natalie stepped up to the microphone, clearing her throat as the crowd fell silent.

"Thank you all. It's so nice to see you all here today." Natalie began, stealing a glance down to her speech cards. She scanned one briefly and continued, "On behalf of Lord and Lady Ragion, my parents, I'd like to thank everyone who…" her voice caught in her throat. The silence was deafening as her mind reeled. She couldn't continue with this false speech. The speech cards slipped out of her fingers, fluttering gently to the floor. Natalie smiled a weak smile to the people gathered before her.

"You know what? This isn't right." she stated, her voice surprisingly sure. "I can't do this anymore." she said, locking eyes with Ian, who returned her gaze in utter bewilderment. "Ladies and gentlemen of the press, I am not…"

Suddenly, the back doors of the ballroom burst open loudly as Lord and Lady Deuhurst came storming in with a girl about Natalie's age in tow.

"Oh by all means, continue my dear. I'd absolutely love to hear what possible excuse you could have for yourself." Lord Deuhurst called out. The crowd's puzzlement was palpable as the murmurs began to circulate around the crowded room.

"Lord Deuhurst, what is the meaning of this outburst?" Lord Granville asked, stepping back to the microphone.

"Ah, yes! The ever faithful friend of the Ragions to the rescue. As if you didn't know the truth." snapped Deuhurst, his wife clinging to his arm, smiling maliciously. "Go ahead, George. Explain to the good people of the press how you manipulated your deceased friend's last will and testament for your own personal benefit."

The crowd gasped at the accusation as Lady Granville clasped a hand to her mouth in horror. Her husband stood still in shock. Lord Deuhurst continued up onto the stage, bearing a manila envelope. He neatly stepped in front of Lord Granville waving the envelope like a weapon before the audience.

"I have here proof of a rather nasty little scandal involving London's own little sweetheart here." he announced, eyeing Natalie ominously. Natalie stood frozen, unsure of what to do. Why was he doing this? She had trusted the Deuhursts and yet here they stood betraying her and incriminating the Granvilles as well!

"This is outrageous!" shouted Lord Granville, trying to reclaim the platform, but Lord Deuhurst held fast, extending a hand towards Natalie.

"Would you step forward, my dear?" he asked. Slowly, Natalie complied and stepped forward. "Now, for the benefit of the crowd before us today, will you please answer me this; are *you* Miss Natalie Ragion, heir to the Ragion Estate?" Lord Deuhurst asked pointedly. Natalie's mouth seemed to go dry as she searched for her voice. Her eyes scanned the great room. All over, people's faces held a sense of expectancy, waiting for her to redeem herself. She stared down at Ian who looked shocked and insulted. His eyes seemed to plead with her to put an end to this nonsense.

"I...I..." she stuttered.

"Speak up, girl." edged Deuhurst.

"No. No, I'm not." Natalie said softly into the microphone.

The frenzy that followed was overwhelming. Reporters called out questions, cameras took endless shots, and television reporters chattered rapidly into their microphones. But the one person Natalie noticed was Ian. First disbelief, then indignation swept over his face. Lord Deuhurst waved a hand for silence, calming the chaotic crowd.

"Care to explain your situation then, Miss?" he sneered. Natalie took a deep breath, sweeping a strand of hair back from her face.

"My name *is* Natalie. But my last name is Rashion. My friends and I arrived in London four weeks ago on a summer trip. Due to a mistake in pronunciation of my last name, I was mistaken for the heiress Natalie Ragion. At first, we thought it might be fun to see how long it would take for everyone to realize the mistake, but everything seemed to get mixed up, and we ended up keeping up the pretenses. I just assumed that the *real* Natalie would show up, and everything would be explained. I never expected to be so readily accepted by everyone." she explained, her voice pleading for understanding. "I told Lord and Lady Deuhurst, and they promised that once they located the real Natalie they would explain everything. Clearly, the Deuhursts, like me, are not what they seem." she snapped, turning to the Deuhursts.

"Oh that's rich. Blame us?" he laughed. "You did nothing of the sort. My wife and I knew from the moment we met you that you couldn't possibly be Natalie. But we had to be sure, so thanks to Scotland Yard, we were able to track down young Miss Ragion and bring her here today." replied Lord Deuhurst. At that, Lady Deuhurst approached her husband with the young girl at her side.

"Hey there you lot." called out the girl, holding her fingers up, making the peace symbol. The cameras clicked again in a frenzy.

Natalie took a good look at the girl whom she had impersonated for so long. The differences were remarkable. True, they both were of the same age and the same general weight and height. Their hair too was similar in color, but there the similarities ended. While Natalie looked coiffed and refined, the other Natalie looked careless and sloppy. She wore a dark, faded black leather jacket overtop a purple and black t-shirt with a band's name splashed over the front. She wore grungy black jeans tattered with holes designed to make them look fashionable, but really looking shabby. Her ears were covered with multiple earrings, and her hair, what little that wasn't brown, was streaked with long purple tips. She wore heavy eye shadow and gaudy black lipstick. Her nails were painted black and she wore cut off gloves with her fingers peeping out. In truth, she was a party girl of the wildest kind. Rich, refined heiress? Definitely not! Natalie couldn't help but feel contempt for her as she now compared the two.

"It's like the Deuhursts said. On my return trip from the old USA, I got a little sidetracked with bunch of friends from Germany. And the lot of us headed for a little trip to the tropics for some sun." chattered the girl in her heavy British accent. Judging from the pallor of this girl's skin, Natalie didn't think she had seen much sun in decades. "Now, I come home here, and find this little American upstart trying to take over my fortune that *my* Mummy and Daddy left for me. If it weren't for the Deuhursts, she'd have made off with the whole kit and caboodle!" she exclaimed, clearly outraged.

"Can you believe this?" Lord Deuhurst declared loudly, riling up the already anxious crowd. "It's clear now that Lord and Lady Granville had purely mercenary motivations in usurping the will and the fortune away from Miss Ragion." The crowd began their murmuring again, as questions were shouted and accusations made.

"That's a lie, Deuhurst! We did nothing of the kind. We had no idea this wasn't really Neville and Luciana's daughter." Lord Granville attempted to win back some of his credibility.

Lord Deuhurst arched an eyebrow, "Did you even bother to check? Or were you too intent on reaping their fortune, stooping as low as using your own son to seduce this imposter and marry them off, thus giving you full access to the money so long protected by the will?"

Natalie pushed her way forward, gripping the microphone tightly in hand.

"Listen to me!" she almost shouted, "Lord and Lady Granville had nothing to do with this. I deceived them. They had no reason to doubt who I said I was. And for my own deception, I've brought embarrassment to them and their family." she declared. The crowd grew silent. "Lord and Lady Granville, please believe me when I say how terribly sorry I am. For all of this. I want to apologize to everyone. I never meant to hurt anyone." she begged, her eyes filling with tears. She turned to look at the other Natalie. "Miss Ragion, I could never be you. I only wanted to know how it *felt* to be you, even if only for a little while." she turned back to the crowd. "I am so sorry." she said as she stared at Ian.

Ian shook his head, dropping a small velvet black box to the floor as he stalked from the room. Natalie felt the tears trickle down her face as the web of lies she had spun unraveled all around her.

"Touching, but not good enough. I'm afraid the police don't take kindly to impersonation and identity theft." crooned Lady Deuhurst in her ear. As if on cue, a small group of policemen marched up the edge of the room and onto the platform.

"Miss Rashion, you're under arrest." the officer stated coldly.

Lady Granville stifled a sob as Natalie followed the lead officer with a group of officers behind her. She spotted James and Michael looking baffled and hurt, and she mouthed an apology to them. With every step, the invasive photographers snapped her picture. She was sure to make the headlines now.

Just then, Grace and Lizzie were racing down the hall having managed to pick the lock on the door with a bobby-pin. They knew they had to hurry and warn Natalie that Lady Deuhurst planned on exposing all of them to the press! As they raced toward the top of the stairs, they heard the din of the crowd below in the ballroom.

"Uh oh. Things sound like their heating up." Lizzie commented.

"Better hurry then." Grace insisted. "Here, this is faster." she added, throwing a leg over the polished banister.

"Grace, what are you *doing*!" demanded Lizzie. But Grace merely smiled mischievously and slid down the banister, rapidly gaining speed. Just as she came towards the end, she unceremoniously fell off in a heap on the floor.

"Okay, that only works in movies." she groaned, rubbing her sore backside. Lizzie shook her head laughing as she met up with Grace at the bottom of the stairs. They both rushed into the room just as the mob came pouring out behind Natalie and an entourage of policemen.

"What on earth?" Lizzie gasped.

"Ah, her cohorts!" Lord Deuhurst pointed out to the policemen. "Officer, these two as well." he insisted. Two of the officers broke off and headed for the girls. Grace instantly turned on her heel to leave.

"Time to go!" she announced taking a step for the door, but Elizabeth grabbed her arm and held her back as the officers herded the two of them along with Natalie.

"Guess the crowd didn't take your explanation very well, huh?" whispered Elizabeth as they marched along.

"It didn't help that the Deuhursts threw me to the wolves *and* produced the real Natalie at the same time." she replied.

Back on the platform, Lord and Lady Granville were left standing in utter embarrassment as the crowd left the room. Lord Deuhurst returned to the room with a satisfied smile on his face.

"Why, Harold? Why would you do this?" Lord Granville asked in a quiet exasperated tone.

Lord Deuhurst turned to stare incredulously. "Why? Why, you ask? The money. Plain and simple. Neville Ragion was my step-brother, and half that inheritance is rightfully mine! If it hadn't been for you and your simpering wife, I'd have been put in charge of his estate, not you. The money would have been divided between me and the girl. But instead, I was simply forgotten, and you were put in charge. We couldn't have that now, could we?" he quipped. The real Natalie sat oblivious in the corner head banging to the music from her ear-phones.

"But that American girl did nothing wrong." insisted Lady Granville.

"Yes, but sacrifices must be made. She was simply in the wrong place, impersonating the wrong person at the right time. She was expendable." replied Deuhurst. "Besides, she'll get off easily enough. I'm sure my darling niece won't press charges, and the authorities will see to it that Miss Rashion is returned to the States, and all will be right again." he assured them. "Oh, with the exception that young Lady Ragion has insisted that I take over as power of attorney instead of you, Lord Granville. So you're free to go."

Lord Granville quietly placed his arm around his wife and in humiliation and anger, silently stepped down from the platform and left the room. The Deuhursts meanwhile rejoiced in their marvelous triumph, while Natalie sat by looking bored.

## Chapter 11

The holding cell was cold and sterile as the three girls sat quietly on the bench, awaiting any changes in their situation. After several hours, Grace began to whimper, trembling as she rocked back and forth on the bench.

"Grace, it's going to be all right. We haven't done anything terribly wrong. I'm sure that once everything is cleared up, they'll let us go home." assured Lizzie, hugging Grace.

But Grace simply shook her head as she cried, "No. No they won't, Lizzie. They're probably just waiting till dawn to take us out and have us executed!" she exclaimed hysterically. "By tomorrow morning, we could all end up like a trio of Henry the eighth's wives! Their guillotine is just waiting for us, I know it." she moaned.

"Only Anne Boleyn was beheaded, Grace." Natalie responded automatically, her voice even and unenthused. "And the guillotine was only used in France." This managed to calm Grace somewhat as the trio returned to their silence.

After a while, all three girls managed to doze off into a fitful sleep. Grace had terrible dreams of dramatic executions with Henry the eighth sentencing her to death in a variety of ways, while Lizzie dreamed of France and James speaking fluent French to her. She was so frustrated that she couldn't understand what he was saying. But Natalie's dreams were merely a replay of that previous afternoon's embarrassment over and over again. She continually saw the hurt in Ian's eyes as he left the room. And although she never got to see what was in the little black velvet box, somehow she knew it had been a ring.

"Alright ladies, you're free to go." a loud female voice announced, waking the girls from their dreams.

"We're doomed." gasped Grace, sitting up suddenly. She blinked her eyes a bit before realizing that she had been dreaming. "Wait, what?" she asked.

"You lot have been let go. It seems there will be no charges pressed. But you are to leave London immediately." the female cop instructed. The girls hastily followed after the woman as she led them out of the holding cell and into the building's lobby. "Your bags have been packed and are waiting for you on a flight bound to the US in one hour." she continued.

"But who…" began Natalie, confused.

Just then she spotted Lord Granville. He looked tired and worn, and his clothes were disheveled. She noticed that he was still wearing the same suit as yesterday.

"Hello girls." he greeted politely, smiling.

"Lord Granville, did you arrange our release?" Natalie asked quickly.

"Let's just say that I don't think Miss Ragion has any reason to press charges. It seems everyone's gotten either what they want or what they deserve." he replied, his voice tinted with bitterness.

Natalie hugged Lord Granville tightly, "Lord Granville, I am so sorry about everything." she whispered.

He smiled, hugging her back and nodding his head. "I know, my dear. I know."

"How's Ian?" she asked tentatively. But at the mention of Ian, Lord Granville became quiet.

"I've got a taxi waiting outside. I'll accompany the three of you to the airport. We'd better hurry if you're going to make your flight." he instructed.

Once in the taxi, Natalie pressed for information about Ian, but Lord Granville merely shook his head sadly.

"I'm sorry dear, but Ian has nothing to say. I saw him briefly last night, but he slipped out very early this morning, and I've not seen or heard from him since."

"When you do see him, please tell him how sorry I am. I never meant to hurt him and I tried to tell him the truth, but I never got the chance." Natalie explained, sadly.

"Perhaps its better this way. The two of you will always be able to look back on this summer and the fond memories you shared. Maybe that's all we can expect from life. Perhaps we're only given short bits of happiness to cling to amidst everything else. It's those good memories that keep us going. I know my wife and I will never forget you. In fact, I can't help but wish you *were* Natalie Ragion. You'd certainly have made Neville and Luciana proud." sighed Lord Granville heavy hearted. Natalie nodded, turning to stare out the window as her tears slid silently down her face.

"Out of curiosity, what will happen to James Butler and Michael Masterly?" Lizzie asked at length.

"Well, if they'd like, they may continue on in Miss Ragion's service. But I've a feeling that with the whole stink of scandal surrounding this affair, they'll probably move on to other prospects. I'll give them your regards though." he assured her. She nodded in response, squeezing Grace's hand gently. She knew Grace was missing Michael, and she felt the pain at not being able to say goodbye to James herself.

All too soon, goodbyes were said, and the girls were whisked through security and seated on the plane. All the while, Natalie said nothing, staring vacantly out the window at the tarmac as the plane was prepped for take off. The gloomy London fog seemed to drag her further into depression.

"Nat, are you going to be all right?" Grace asked hesitantly.

Natalie turned and smiled at her cousin and her friend. "Yeah, I'll be fine. I just need some time." she replied, then added, "This will definitely be one summer I'll never forget. And despite it all, I'm glad I got to spend it with you guys. I love you both. You're the best friends anyone could ask for."

"We *are* pretty awesome." Lizzie jokingly agreed. The pilot's voice interrupted and then Natalie remained silent for the remainder of the flight, feeling empty as she watched London slip away beneath her.

\*\*\*\*\*\*\*\*\*

The rest of their summer passed by as summers typically do; busy with work and what not, and wishing that the long, hot days would never end. The girls saw less of each other due to job obligations and schedule conflicts, but they still tried to make time for each other. Of course there was the matter of explaining to their parents what had *actually* happened on the trip, which resulted in a very *long* lecture the girls were sure never to forget. But even through it all, Natalie couldn't seem to shake her depression. She missed Ian. Missed his smile, his laughter, and his blue eyes. And she hated not knowing what might have been had she just been upfront and honest with him. Her parents did their best to try and distract her from thinking of him, and while she appreciated their efforts, it was all in vain. Something deep inside her didn't want to forget Ian. She knew that these depressing thoughts of him were all the proof she had left that she had felt anything for him at all. Some days she would let her mind wander back through all the good times they had spent in London or at his summer home. Other days, she would get indignant and angry at him for not understanding her situation. It was on such a day as this that Grace and Elizabeth decided to visit their despondent friend and attempt to cheer her up.

The sky was dark and rain was pouring down as Grace knocked at the door and was greeted by her aunt, Natalie's mom, who showed the girls in.

"How's Natalie doing?" Lizzie asked hesitantly.

Mrs. Rashion sighed and shook her head, "The same, I'm afraid. She just keeps sitting around gloomily, thinking about that boy from London."

"I had hoped she'd be over it all by now." Grace admitted.

"Her dad and I had hoped this was just some summer romance, a puppy love so to speak. But I think now it may have been a bit deeper."

The girls agreed, knowing how much in love Natalie and Ian had been, and how hurt both must have felt upon the end of the trip.

"She's in her room watching a movie." Mrs. Rashion pointed out. The girls thanked her and headed off for Natalie's room. As they poked their heads through the door they saw Natalie slumped on her bed wearing sweatpants and a big sweatshirt with the hood pulled tightly over her head. She looked tired and grumpy as she stared at her TV.

"Watcha watching, Nat?" Grace asked tentatively.

"A movie."

"I can see that. Which one?"

"*An Affair to Remember*. It's dumb."

Elizabeth slid onto the bed next to Natalie, "So why are you watching it then?" she asked.

"Nothing else to do." Natalie replied in a bored voice.

The girls watched as the climax of the movie approached and the two lovers who refused to speak finally resolved their differences as the music swelled and the tears flowed. The lovers kissed passionately, declaring their love.

"YOU'RE AN IDIOT!" shouted Natalie suddenly at the movie. "Love is a fake! You lied to him and he won't forgive you! Your happily ever after won't come true!" she continued shouting. Grace and Elizabeth stared wide-eyed at their friend who suddenly hushed her vehement declaration against love.

"Um..." Elizabeth began.

"Looks like the movie's over." Grace muttered.

Natalie sighed, sinking back on her pillow. "Sorry guys. I guess I'm just not able to get over this." she confessed. "Love stinks."

"Yeah, it does sometimes. But you know what, Nat?" Elizabeth asked. Natalie looked up at her friend waiting for words of encouragement. "Sometimes you just gotta get up, and *move on*!" she exclaimed. "I mean, gosh, Nat. It's been two months since London. I understand you miss Ian and you're upset at how things turned out, but are you really gonna let this eat your lunch?" she demanded.

"Ooh, lunch! I'm gonna go see if there's something to eat." Grace announced making for the kitchen.

Natalie heaved a big sigh, pulling herself upright. "No." she mumbled.

"And are you really going to sit around for the rest of your summer? I mean, in a few weeks we'll all be heading off for college. A fresh page, a new start. Life is moving on. Don't just watch it go by, make it happen!" challenged Lizzie forcefully. "Now, you're going to get up and change into something other than sweats, and the three of us are going to gorge ourselves on ice cream while we talk college plans."

Natalie smiled at her friend and impulsively threw her arms around her and hugged her.

"Alright general. Lead the way." she laughed.

"Oh, by the way, we've got news." Grace announced munching on a cookie. "Lookie here." she held up a paper printed from the computer. It appeared to be a headline of sorts. Natalie took it and read: *Scandal Erupts over Party Girl Heiress Natalie Ragion*. She quickly scanned down reading the article that went on to explain how that while in America, Natalie Ragion had been nothing but a jet-setting party girl who had racked up millions in debts, easily dwarfing her father's inheritance. She was now being forced to sell everything at auction just to pay off her debts. The Deuhursts, who had claimed responsibility for finding her, now wanted nothing to do with her. The Granvilles had nothing to comment due to their recent embarrassment with the mistaken identity of the American imposter.

"You've got to admit. That's a pretty fitting end to both Natalie and the Deuhursts." Lizzie commented. Natalie shook her head in agreement, crumpling up the paper and forcing it from her mind.

A week went by, and Natalie's mood improved. She grabbed life by the horns. She went out, instead of moping in her room for hours on end. She ate proper meals instead of canned goods with a spoon. Her parents silently rejoiced at the emergence of their daughter once again. They were so happy in fact, that they decided to go out for the day to celebrate, leaving Natalie to herself for the first time since her depression.

"Now are you sure you're going to be alright by yourself?" her dad asked for the millionth time.

"Yes, Dad. I'll be fine. I've got a frozen pizza, a stack of movies, and several more stacks of college paperwork to fill out. You two go and have fun." she urged. Her dad kissed her forehead.

"I love you, sweetie."

"Love you too, Dad." she replied.

With that, her parents drove off for an enjoyable day out while Natalie headed for the paperwork. The day was surprisingly muggy, with the humidity levels high. Natalie fanned herself, longing for August to be over. She was ready for the changing of leaves that September would bring, and the cool autumn air that came with it. She mopped at the sweat on the back of her neck. With her fingers cramping up from continuous writing, Natalie decided that a break and a cool down were in order. She headed off for the bathroom where she proceeded to dowse her head in a sink of cold water.

Just then, a loud knock at the door grabbed her attention.

"Of course. Someone *would* interrupt me while my hair's soaking wet." she muttered, wrapping a towel around her head like a turban and going for the front door. As she swung the door open, she almost passed out. There on her front porch, looking terribly nervous and slightly bemused was Ian!

"Um…hi. Sorry, I should've called." he apologized, his hands shoved deep in his pockets as he shifted nervously from foot to foot.

"Oh my gosh! Ian! What…how…what are you doing here?" she asked bluntly, one hand frozen in place on the door handle, the other keeping her towel turban from falling off.

"Well, it's kind of a long story. Is…it alright if I come in?" he asked carefully.

"Yeah! I mean, sure." Natalie gestured for him to enter as she suddenly realized that her hair was dripping wet and she looked like an idiot with a towel wrapped around her head. "I'm sorry about this," she pointed at the towel, "You caught me just as I was drying my hair."

"Oh no its fine." he insisted. The two of them sat down in the living room, not saying a word.

"Look I've just gotta say…" they both spoke at once. Natalie laughed as Ian smiled. Oh, how she remembered that smile.

"You first." he offered.

"Ian, I am so sorry." she began. "I never meant to lie to you and hurt you the way I did. In fact, I tried to meet you that last morning to tell you the truth, but I was detained by Lord Deuhurst. And at the airport your dad said he hadn't seen you since the night before, and it tore me up not being able to speak with you personally. I've been a wreck ever since." she confessed, lowering her face, not daring to look Ian in the eyes. But Ian gently tilted her chin up to face him as he smiled down at her.

"Natalie, its alright." he stated simply. Natalie felt suddenly very flushed as she smiled back.

"Oh okay." she replied.

Ian leaned in and kissed her. "I'm in love with you, and I'm the one who should be apologizing. I made a fool of myself the whole time. Acting like some love-struck idiot, spouting stupid lines to you trying to impress you. I even bought a…" he stopped himself. But Natalie smiled. "You knew, didn't you?" he asked.

"Well, there are only so many things that come in small black jewelry boxes, Ian." she admitted. He laughed, hugging her to him.

"Like I said before, I can be a little impulsive."

"That's one of the things I like about you." Natalie sighed. Suddenly, she pulled away her face a mask of confusion. "But how did you get here? And how did you find me?" she asked puzzled.

"After you left, my father told me what you said. He explained for you, and told me that I was acting like a spoiled brat to think that you were totally in the wrong. Well, after much soul-searching and several days spent moping around my parent's summer home, I decided that I didn't care what it took; I had to find you again. Because my life is and always will be empty without you in it." he declared. "So, I hopped on a flight, found out where the state of Michigan was, looked up your parents' names and drove here. Not an easy thing to do, by the way, for a guy who drives on the opposite side of the road. I may have almost hit your postman on my way in." he laughed. Natalie looked up at Ian lovingly.

"That is the sweetest thing I've ever heard." she sighed.

"Really? Because I've never thought of almost hitting someone with an automobile terribly romantic." he replied. She laughed as she undid the towel on her head, pulling her wet hair into a ponytail. "But seriously though, Natalie, wherever you are, that's where I want to be too." His face grew serious, "Which is why, as of this September, I will be attending college here in the States with you." he announced. Natalie squealed, throwing her arms around his neck and kissing his face repeatedly. This much good news in one day just had to be too good to be true!

"Wait, what about James and Michael?" she asked suddenly.

"Don't you worry about them. As we speak, they are making their way to the respective homes of Grace and Elizabeth with some good news of their own. James managed to get a job teaching French at a school here in the States. And Michael has also wrangled a security job nearby in the hopes of being closer to Grace. So, all in all, I'd say that's a pretty good end to everything." he agreed. "Natalie, I promise you this time, we'll do things right. If ever I start moving too fast, you stop me. I don't want to mess this up and risk losing you again." he insisted. But Natalie shook her head and leaned in for a kiss.

"I love you, Ian. I have since that night we met on the bridge. Now I don't know what the future has in store for us, but let's just enjoy this little trip called life, one precious moment at a time."

"Sounds like a plan to me, Miss Ragion." he stated, leaning in.

"Its Rashion." she corrected, smiling.

"I knew that." he whispered. And the two kissed once more.

# The End

# Would you like to see your manuscript become a book?

If you are interested in becoming a PublishAmerica author, please submit your manuscript for possible publication to us at:

**acquisitions@publishamerica.com**

You may also mail in your manuscript to:

**PublishAmerica
PO Box 151
Frederick, MD 21705**

## We also offer free graphics for Children's Picture Books!

**www.publishamerica.com**

**PublishAmerica**